CYBERINTELLIGENCE

VLADIMIR LUGO

CYBERINTELLIGENCE

5 TRANSFORMATIONS

ARTIFICIAL INTELLIGENCES FACILITATES IN THE CHURCH

SERIES: CYBERMINISTRY **6**

CYBERINTELLIGENCE

5 Transformations Artificial Intelligence Facilitates in the Church

vladimir@vladimirlugo.com
www.vladimirlugo.com

Published in the United States of America
by Tepui Media, LLC, Sheridan, Wyoming

ISBN-13 Paperback: 979-8-9884611-8-0
ISBN-13 Electronic: 979-8-9884611-9-7

Library of Congress Control Number: 2025912808

Other resources by Vladimir Lugo

Cyberminister Today
Receive my articles where I explore the topic of using technology in ministry and receive notifications about new publications, conferences, and seminars right in the comfort of your email inbox. Visit www.vladimirlugo.com.

#tecnologiasministeriales | #cyberministry | #cyberintelligence

Follow me **@vladimirlugomt** and join the conversation in social media.

Dedication

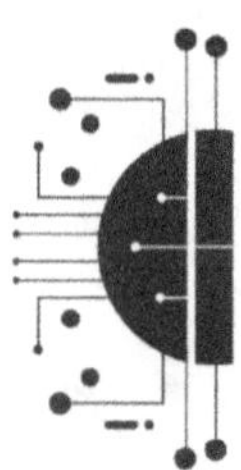

Give thanks to the Lord of lords:
His love endures forever,
who by his understanding made the
heavens, His love endures forever.

– Psalms 136:3,5

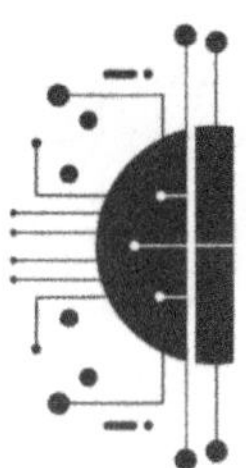

Today, after more than a century of electric technology, we have extended our central nervous system itself in a global embrace.

– Marshal McLuhan

TABLE OF FIGURES

Figure 1: Artificial Intelligence Layers

Figure 2: Ministerial Technologies Matrix®

Figure 4: The DICTS Model

TABLE OF CONTENT

Dedication vii

Table of figures xi

Table of Content xiii

Preface xix

Profiling Technology xx

Ministry and Technology xxi

Why Artificial Intelligence xxiii

Why this Book xxv

Who Should Read this Book? xxvi

How to Use this Book xxviii

Introduction to AI 3

Innovation and Religion 5

Definition and Basic Concepts 8

Narrow AI vs. Strong AI 12

AI and Society 13

The Church in the Digital Age 17

The Digital Era 19

Innovation in Tradition 22

Ministerial Technologies 24

In was the Beginning the Word 27

Prompt Engineering 30

The DICTS Model 31

Cyberintelligent Adoring **35**

More than Sounds and Aesthetics 38

Altar Allies 39

Spectators More Than Participants 44

Augmented, Not Replaced, Worship 45

An Altar Without Artifice 46

Cyberintelligent Assimilating **49**

Prepare Intelligently, Preach Wisely 51

Classrooms That Learn 55

Dethroning Babel 58

Learning with Humility 61

Cyberintelligent Announcing **65**

An Eternal Message for an Encrypted World 68

New Public Squares 70

Evangelists at the Digital Door 75

Missional Strategy 77

The Universal Key 81

Cyberintelligent Assisting **85**

Vision and Pastoral Presence 87

Pastoral Ally 90

Crisis Management 93

Compassion and Justice with AI 95

Seeing Better to Help Better 98

Cyberintelligent Associating **101**

Beyond Fellowship 103

Organize for Better Care 106

Freeing your Schedule to Embrace your Neighbor 109
When Automation is Caring 110
Shepherding Without Getting Trapped in Administration 111
When Coordinating is Loving 115

Cyberintelligent Wisdom & Ethics 119

Creative Aid or Illusion of the Prophetic 121
Creative dependency 123
Ethical Collection and Use of Data 125
Can AI help? Yes – if it learns from our ethics 128
Dehumanization and Algorithmic Biases 129
Discerning is not Predicting 132
Biblical wisdom as a guiding principle 134
Technological governance 137

Technology & Faith in the Age of AI 141

Technology is not neutral 143
Redemption and Tension 147
Instruments of Mission 149
The Idolatry of Efficiency 153
Redemption of the Tool 155
From the Shadows of the Thunderhead 157

Strategic Challenges of AI 159

The Horologium of Richard of Wallingford 160
The Clock as a Pastoral Symbol 164
Prioritizing the Eternal Amidst the Immediate 166
Vision, Resources, and Resistance 169
Proactive Leadership 170

Cybermaturity as a Guide 172
Governance, Accountability, and Witness 173

A Look into the Future 177

What will you leave behind? 179
The Future Among Us 180
Risks and Opportunities 182
Final Recommendations 187
Firm Hope 189

AI Applications 193

Applications Classified by Categories 195
Write Your Book Using IA 200

Appendix A: Glossary 209

Appendix B: Discussion Questions 213

Chapter 1: Introduction to IA 213
Chapter 2: The Church in the Digital Age 214
Chapter 3: Cyberintelligent Adoring 214
Chapter 4: Cyberintelligent Assimilating 215
Chapter 5: Cyberintelligent Announcing 216
Chapter 6: Cyberintelligent Assisting 216
Chapter 7: Cyberintelligent Associating 217
Chapter 8: Cyberintelligent Wisdom & Ethics 218
Chapter 9: Technology & Faith in the Age of AI 218
Chapter 10: Strategic Challenges of AI 219
Chapter 11: A Look into the Future 219
Chapter 12: IA Applications 220

Acknowledgements **221**

Consulting Services **223**

About the Series **225**

About the Author **227**

Limitation of Liability **231**

Bibliography **233**

Printed 233

Online 234

Annotations **237**

PREFACE

Artificial Intelligence
is the new electricity.

– ANDREW NG, INFORMATION SCIENTIST.

I had just graduated from seminary in the year 2000 when a software development company hired me as Director of Research. At first, the title struck me as a bit odd – perhaps because I did not fully understand the nature of the job – but I was soon about to find out.

The company, a research subsidiary of NBC (the broadcasting network), was focused on finding a niche that would allow us to break into the dot-com world. We were creating a marketing software product with the potential to eventually help us take the company public on the New York Stock Exchange.

As Director of Research, my job was to prove that the software under development worked and delivered on its promise. To do that, I had to organize focus groups with volunteer users who would test the software, while we collected real-time data through the same system to later analyze the results. After several rounds of testing and close to a thousand participants, we had enough proof to present the product to potential investors. The software was a resounding success.

We participated in several live demos to showcase the software in action – many of them met with amazement. I clearly remember one of the most anticipated presentations: a session with the executives from Blockbuster. For those who may not know or remember, Blockbuster was the world's leading company for renting VHS movie tapes and compact music discs at the time.

The Blockbuster executives were deeply impressed by the results. I even recall the company president engaging in a lengthy session with our team, trying to anticipate the software's responses – only to be continually surprised by the suggestions the system generated, many of which they had not even considered.

A few days later, we learned that Blockbuster had decided not to move forward with the software. Eventually, we also discovered that they simply were not that interested in innovation – a mindset that ultimately pushed them out of the market in the face of emerging competitors like Netflix and Redbox. They missed a golden opportunity – one that might have saved them from bankruptcy.

Profiling Technology

The software in my story was what we now know as *profiling technology*. The company I worked for was a pioneer in developing this kind of technology, which has since become an integral part of user experiences across many software platforms.

Profiling technology refers to the process of collecting, analyzing, and using data to create detailed profiles of individuals, groups, or entities. This type of technology is commonly used in marketing, online advertising, security, social media applications, and other areas where understanding and predicting human behavior is essential.

Technology-driven profiling can include personal information, preferences, online behavior, browsing history, social media interactions, and other relevant data that help construct an accurate and comprehensive user profile.

The software will use the user's profile to offer recommendations that closely match the user's preferences, with the goal of reinforcing expected behavior. Think of Amazon recommending your next purchase, Netflix anticipating what you will want to watch next, or American Express alerting you to a potentially fraudulent transaction because it does not match your usual spending pattern.

Artificial intelligence (AI) makes all these things possible – or more precisely, to certain layers of AI, particularly those related to deep learning and machine learning. I will not get overly technical here (though I will provide a foundation in Chapter 1), but it is worth noting that AI is not a brand-new development. It has evolved gradually, gaining major traction and practical application over the past 25 years, especially with the rise of the Internet.

Profiling technology depends on AI and related tools that can rapidly analyze and process the vast amounts of data involved. AI is applied to identify patterns, trends, and correlations within massive data sets, enabling the creation of more accurate and detailed profiles. In addition, AI can automate the entire data analysis process, making it possible to build and update user profiles continuously and in real time.

Ministry and Technology

In my previous books, *Cyberministry* and *Cybermaturity*, I laid the foundation for how technology can be used in the ministry of the church. If you're not familiar with those concepts, I encourage you to explore them, as they provide a valuable basis for what I'm about to share in the following pages.

Cyberministry explores five essential functions of technology through the strategic lens of the church's mission. It offers both a clear framework and practical guidance for making the most of available technological tools – especially in the wake of the recent pandemic and lockdowns, which forced the church to face an unprecedented wave of digital transformation.

Cybermaturity, on the other hand, serves as a unique guide to technological maturity in Christian ministry and pastoral work. It walks you through seven practical steps to help ensure that ministry technologies bear lasting fruit. The book is filled with actionable advice on how to assess your digital programs and make sure they are delivering the results you expect. Both books are valuable resources for church leaders seeking to integrate technology into their ministries in an effective and fruitful way.

Technology has been a transformative force throughout history, and the church has never been relieved from these technological shifts, often even leading the way in some cases.

In today's digital era, the role of technology in the church has become more visible than ever

In today's digital era, the role of technology in the church has become more visible than ever, opening new pathways for communication, community, and worship. It's within this broader framework that artificial intelligence presents unique opportunities for Christian ministry.

AI offers the potential for greater communication efficiency and outreach in our efforts to share the Gospel, along with more personalized engagement and messages that are deeply informed by their cultural and social context.

But before we go any further, let us be clear: artificial intelligence is a tool – just like any other technology we already use. Like any other tool, it brings both challenges and opportunities, and it must be evaluated through the same lens of practical and ethical scrutiny.

AI is already embedded in the everyday lives of ordinary people, even if we do not always recognize it or identify it by name.

Why Artificial Intelligence

I want to anticipate several reasons why we are encouraged – if not compelled – to explore artificial intelligence and its application to ministry.

Enriching Worship and Education

Artificial intelligence can help you create more interactive and immersive worship experiences, as well as provide adaptive learning platforms for Christian education and spiritual formation. This can enhance engagement and improve retention of biblical knowledge. I explore this in **Chapter 3** and **Chapter 4**.

Improved Communication and Outreach

AI tools can assist in crafting communication plans, enhancing the preaching experience, generating email campaigns, or translating church sermons and materials into multiple languages – both written and spoken. This increases relevance and allows the church's message to reach a global audience. I will discuss these ideas in **Chapter 5** and **Chapter 9**.

Administrative Efficiency

Artificial intelligence can automate administrative tasks such as donation tracking, event planning, and volunteer coordination, freeing up time for ministers to focus on pastoral care and community development. It can also assist in analyzing financial data and other metrics, building presentations, and organizing information in creative ways. You will find out more about this in **Chapter 7**.

Decision-Making Support

Through predictive analytics, AI can help church leaders make informed decisions about church growth, resource allocation, and evangelism strategies. I also address this in **Chapter 7**.

Personalizing the Spiritual Journey

AI can process large datasets to better understand the needs and preferences of church members, allowing pastors and leaders to tailor sermons, Bible studies, and church activities more effectively. I explore this partially in **Chapter 6.**

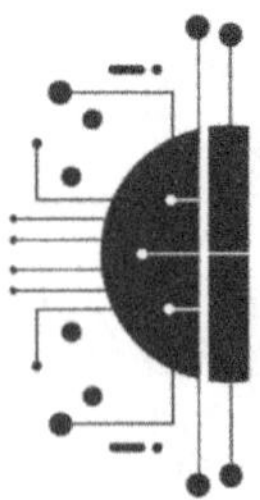

Technological innovation enables us to adapt our traditions to a contemporary context—making the message more accessible and relevant

Innovation within Tradition

While the church deeply values its theological and liturgical traditions, technological innovation enables us to adapt our traditions to a contemporary context – making the message more accessible and relevant to current generations without compromising sound doctrine or faith and conduct standards. I cover this topic at length in *Cybermaturity* and touch on it again in **Chapter 2**.

Ministry Expansion

It is well known that technology dissolves or blurs geographic and temporal boundaries, enabling church services and programs to reach those who cannot attend in person. Artificial intelligence is a powerful tool for developing strategies for growth and future expansion, especially when used as a brainstorming assistant to spark creativity among ministry teams. See **Chapter 10** for more details.

Virtual Community

Online platforms powered by AI can help you build and sustain a faith community even when members are physically distant. Automation tools like chatbots (**Chapter 6**) and other virtual assistants can strengthen that sense of connection and belonging.

For these reasons – and many more – it is not plainly important to integrate artificial intelligence into the life of the church; it is essential if ministries are to remain relevant and effective in the 21st century. Artificial intelligence offers ministers powerful tools to enrich spiritual experience, expand Gospel outreach, and manage church communities with greater efficiency. It has become imperative that church leaders actively explore and adopt AI in their ministry practices.

Why this Book

Cyberintelligence: 5 Transformations Artificial Intelligence Facilitates in the Church is a practical guide for exploring the intersection between artificial intelligence and Christian ministry. It offers a comprehensive look at how modern technology can revolutionize traditional church practices.

The book introduces AI as a transformative tool that can enhance multiple areas of ministry – from sermon preparation and pastoral care to evangelism and church administration.

Its main goal is to equip Christian leaders with the understanding and strategies needed to effectively integrate artificial intelligence into their ministries, ensuring they remain relevant and impactful in today's digital age.

Structured around ten core chapters, the book explores key areas of the church's mission where artificial intelligence can make a meaningful difference.

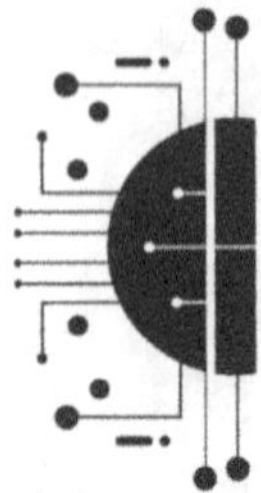

Artificial intelligence is a powerful tool for developing strategies for growth and future expansion

Cyberintelligence begins by laying a foundational understanding of AI: what it is, where it comes from, and how it's already influencing society. From there, it moves into more practical applications, such as using AI tools for preaching, worship, pastoral care, and outreach.

The book does not shy away from the tough questions, either. It tackles the ethical and theological challenges AI presents, encouraging readers to reflect on both the possibilities and the risks of incorporating this technology into spiritual contexts.

Throughout the journey, I emphasize the need to balance innovation with the core values of the Christian faith. The final chapters look ahead to the future of AI in the church, offering strategic recommendations to help church leaders navigate this fast-changing landscape.

By blending theological insight with hands-on guidance, **Cyberintelligence** serves as a valuable resource for anyone seeking to explore how artificial intelligence can be used to advance the mission of the church in the 21st century.

Who Should Read this Book?

Cyberintelligence, following in the footsteps of the *Cyberministry* series, is written for Christian leaders and ministry workers serving in a variety of contexts – churches, mission organizations, parachurch ministries, educational institutions, community service foundations, and even the broader workplace.

Pastors

Those who seek to understand the current moment and design effective strategies rooted in the message of salvation – lead pastors, administrative pastors, and leaders of various ministries – will find in this book a guide to develop a shared vocabulary and clear direction for integrating artificial intelligence into their ministry vision and mission for future generations.

Denominational Leaders

Those tasked with crafting policies and procedures that guide pastors and churches across their networks – regional superintendents, national directors, association leaders, and apostles or "pastors of pastors" – can come together to engage today's challenges around artificial intelligence and shape a comprehensive, ministry-wide vision.

Christian Educators

Those who shape our worldview, disciple our children with Christian values, and prepare future leaders through theological and holistic education. Seminary and Bible college professors, Christian school teachers at every level, and Sunday school or Bible study instructors are uniquely positioned to guide their students – especially in understanding the ethical and practical implications of AI.

Ministry Leaders

Those who faithfully carry out the work of the church each week – worship leaders and musicians, media and sound technicians, evangelism and missions' directors, counselors and social workers, small group facilitators and greeters, as well as administrators and support staff – will find actionable insights to help them increase their impact through the smart use of artificial intelligence.

Every Believer

All who are called to fulfill the Great Commission. Christ's command remains alive today, but it must continually be reimagined to remain relevant and transformative considering technological advancement.

Cyberintelligence offers practical tools for any Christian wanting to leverage AI in their service to others. While the content is firmly rooted in ministry practice, readers in other sectors, whether academic, nonprofit, or corporate, will also find valuable strategies they can apply in their own fields. There is something here for everyone.

How to Use this Book

I wrote Ciberinteligencia with the goal of helping every Christian leader thoughtfully consider and implement artificial intelligence in their ministry. Depending on your specific area of service, you will find practical ideas throughout this book – and even guidance on how to use AI itself to uncover and explore new ideas, using the principles found within these pages.

You can also use this book in the following ways:

As a reference manual

Cyberintelligence can help you design ministry strategies that are either built on or supported by artificial intelligence. This book functions as a reference guide, offering clear direction and real-life examples for using AI in areas such as preaching, evangelism, church administration, and more.

Keep it nearby as a resource to ensure your strategies are grounded in sound knowledge and proven practices – something that will increase your chances of successfully integrating these technologies into your ministry.

As a small group study guide

Use this book to spark group discussions that allow your congregation to collectively explore the role of AI in the church. These conversations can be a powerful way to discern how technology can serve the mission of Christ and help you establish church-wide policies for its use.

It is also a fantastic opportunity to educate and prepare your community for the technological changes ahead, so that everyone aligns themselves with the vision and direction of your church.

As an academic resource in theological education

Incorporating *Cyberintelligence* into seminary or Christian university courses is a timely way to equip the next generation of church leaders.

This book provides a current perspective on artificial intelligence and its implications for ministry, and it gives students the practical and ethical tools they need to navigate future responsibilities with theological depth and real-world wisdom.

As a gateway to additional resources

At the end of the book, you will find an appendix of supplemental resources to deepen your knowledge in specific areas of interest. You will also find a glossary of technical terms used throughout the book to help you better understand AI's functionality and implications.

These resources are also available on the **Cyberministry** website (https://cyberministry.info). There, you will find ongoing updates and new materials. I encourage you to use them to enrich both your reading experience and your ministry practice.

This book is not meant to be exhaustive or final on the topic of AI in the Church. Rather, I intended for it to be a clear, relevant introduction – one that will inspire you to keep learning, experimenting, and imagining what is possible.

I invite you to use this book as a conversation starter – and then reach out to me personally. You will find my contact information in the "**About the Author**" section. Join the book's discussion group on Goodreads (https://goodreads.com/vladimirlugomt) and connect with me on social media using the handle: @vladimirlugomt.

I would love to hear your thoughts. Feel free to reach out privately – or, if you are willing to go the extra mile, leave a review on Amazon once you have finished reading. Your honest feedback helps me serve you better in future editions and upcoming publications on this important topic.

I pray this book helps you make wise, faithful, and effective use of artificial intelligence in ministry – both for your personal growth and for the flourishing of the community you serve.

Expecting remarkable things,

Your servant in Christ,

Vladimir Lugo
Los Angeles, California
August 2024.

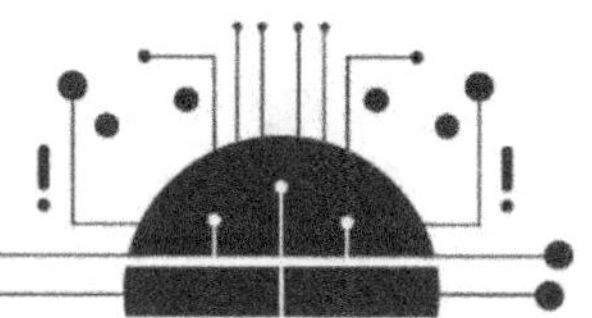

INTRODUCTION TO AI

Artificial intelligence, the science of making machines do things that would require intelligence if done by men. [1]

– MARVIN MINSKY, INFORMATION SCIENTIST.

Hero of Alexandria was one of the most industrious inventors and engineers of antiquity – not only leaving his mark in the fields of mechanics and physics, but also profoundly shaping the religious experience of his time. He lived in the first century A.D., an era when science and religion coexisted in a delicate balance, and his innovative work in creating automatic devices revolutionized temple practices across the Hellenistic world. [2]

In the first-century world – where the early church was just beginning to spread the Gospel – religion was deeply woven into every aspect of daily life. Temples were not just places of worship but also served as community centers where festivals were celebrated, offerings made, and divine guidance sought on important matters. Interacting with the divine was central to both public and private life, and any innovation that could enhance this interaction was warmly welcomed.

Alexandria, where Hero conducted his work, was a melting pot of knowledge and culture. As the intellectual hub of the ancient world, it was home to the famous Library of Alexandria and the Museum, where the era's brightest thinkers gathered. In this climate of intellectual exchange, Hero thrived – bringing his genius to bear on the fusion of science and religious experience.

While Hero is known for a wide range of inventions, his most fascinating creations were tied to automation and its application in religious settings. Among his most notable devices were automata – mechanical constructs capable of performing repetitive tasks autonomously – which were used in temples to create mystical and awe-inspiring experiences for worshippers.

One of Hero's most famous inventions was the automated temple, a structure that combined hydraulic and pneumatic engineering to simulate divine intervention. When a flame was lit on the altar, the temple doors would open automatically – suggesting to onlookers that the god had accepted the offering and was now present. The mechanism operated via a system of counterweights and chains triggered by the heat of the fire, creating a seemingly supernatural effect.

Another remarkable invention was the priest automaton – a mechanical figure capable of performing rituals like pouring libations or moving sacred objects autonomously. These automata were designed to astonish worshippers and reinforce the belief that the gods were actively participating in worship. For priests, these machines enabled precise execution of rituals, heightening the sense of divine presence.

Hero also designed various machines to produce special effects in temples. These included thunder simulators, devices that mimicked the voices of gods, self-operating holy water dispensers, and statues that moved or even "spoke" via compressed air systems. Such mechanical marvels contributed to immersive religious atmospheres where the divine seemed tangibly nearby.

The integration of these mechanisms into temple life profoundly changed how worshippers perceived their connection to the divine. Hero's devices transformed temples into spaces where technology and faith were inseparably entwined, elevating spiritual experience through technological wonder.

In ancient Greece and the broader Hellenistic world, religion was inseparable from spectacle and demonstrations of both divine and human power. Hero's automata amplified this dynamic, enabling temples to stage impressive displays that convinced worshippers of the gods' active presence. Automatically opening doors, talking statues, and mechanically enacted rituals created an environment where the divine became physically manifest.

Hero's inventions also reflect his deep understanding of human psychology. He recognized that perceptions of the miraculous could be shaped by technology, and that awe and wonder could reinforce belief and devotion. In this light, Hero was not only an engineer but also a master of religious persuasion, using technology to deepen spiritual engagement.

Hero's influence extended far beyond his own time. His work was recorded in treatises like *Pneumatica* and *Automata*, which inspired future generations of engineers. Although many of his devices were lost to time, his concepts resurfaced in the Middle Ages and Renaissance, impacting modern engineering.

His religious legacy is seen in the way he foreshadowed future technological innovations in worship – from the mechanical organs of medieval cathedrals to the light and sound spectacles of today's churches. Hero's work shows us that religion and technology are not opposing forces, but powerful partners in shaping sacred experiences.

Innovation and Religion

When considering the work of Hero of Alexandria, it's inevitable to reflect on how his technological innovations might be viewed through the lens of the Christian faith. Although Hero lived within a pagan Hellenistic cultural and religious context – and while his inventions could be categorized as idolatrous in essence (a problem of religion, not of the technology itself) – his ability to use technology to enrich religious experience resonates with current discussions around the use of technology, and artificial intelligence in particular, in Christian ministry. Just as Hero's automata served to enhance the perception of the divine in the temples of his time, today's artificial intelligence presents new possibilities to deepen and expand the church's mission in the modern world.

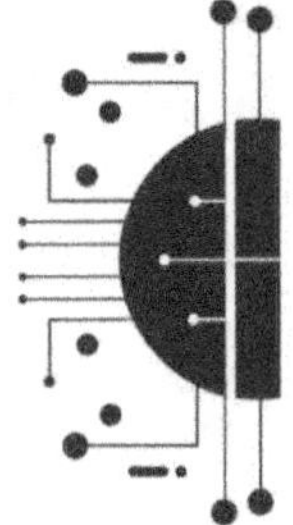

Artificial intelligence presents new possibilities to deepen and expand the church's mission in the modern world

Technology has the power to amplify and extend our human capabilities. In a Christian context, this becomes a powerful tool for ministry – enabling the church not only to remain relevant in an increasingly digital world but also to expand its reach in ways that were once unimaginable.

Hero of Alexandria, though separated from our present reality by centuries, employed similar principles in his own time. His automata and mechanical devices, designed to enhance religious experience, can be seen as precursors to modern artificial intelligence. These machines did not just amaze worshipers – they created a more tangible connection between the human and the divine, a longing that remains central to the Christian faith.

Hero's work invites us to consider how technology can be used to serve faith in ways that are both innovative and reverent. In the temples of the Hellenistic world, his machines functioned as intermediaries between worshipers and their gods, making rituals more impressive and, in some sense, more effective. In a similar way, artificial intelligence in today's church can support evangelism, enhance church administration, and personalize pastoral care – all with the aim of better serving the faith community.

Modern artificial intelligence tools can answer questions about faith, guide new believers in their spiritual journey, and offer real-time support and counsel. These tools could help shoulder some of the more routine demands of ministry.

Just as Hero's devices automated certain aspects of worship – allowing priests to focus on more spiritual responsibilities – AI can streamline administrative tasks such as donation management, event planning, and volunteer coordination. This automation not only makes church operations more efficient but also frees up spiritual leaders to focus on pastoral care, where their presence matters most.

Yet the use of AI in Christian ministry also brings ethical and theological challenges. While Hero's machines were viewed as engineering marvels that brought worshipers closer to their gods, AI – being a modern and complex technology – can often be met with skepticism. It's essential for the church to engage these concerns openly and thoughtfully, ensuring that the use of such tools remains grounded in biblical principles and aligned with the mission of Christ. I will address these issues directly and candidly in **Chapter 8**.

For now, it is important that the church not view artificial intelligence solely as means to make ministry more efficient, but as an opportunity to deepen faith and community. Just as Hero's mechanisms allowed worshipers to experience the divine more tangibly, AI can help create deeper, more meaningful spiritual experiences – through personalized sermons, AI-generated worship music, or even discipleship platforms tailored to individual needs. In any case, there is much work ahead to fully harness these capabilities for the Kingdom.

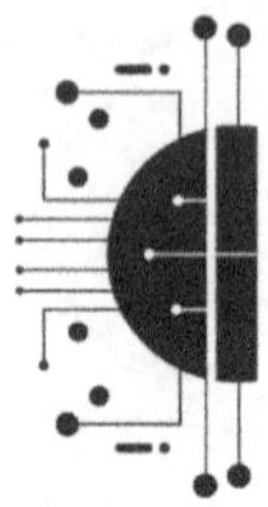

Modern artificial intelligence tools can answer questions about faith

Definition and Basic Concepts

Artificial Intelligence is a science. A development in Information Theory that aims to create systems able to replicate or simulate human cognitive abilities by using algorithms, mathematical models, and massive amounts of data.

Various efforts run in parallel to mimic abilities such as pattern recognition, natural language processing, decision-making and self-learning.

Artificial Intelligence draws on various technological developments and combines them to perform tasks we might consider intelligent. Here, I list eight of them.

Machine Learning

One of the foundational concepts in AI is *machine learning*, a subfield that enables machines to learn from data. Instead of being explicitly programmed to perform a specific task, machine learning systems analyze large datasets, identify patterns, and use those patterns to make decisions or predictions.

Deep Learning

Within machine learning, there is a more advanced technique known as *deep learning*. This approach uses neural networks composed of layers of artificial neurons that process information hierarchically, allowing the system to learn complex and abstract features from raw data. Deep learning has been particularly successful in areas such as speech recognition, computer vision, and natural language processing.

Neural Networks

Neural networks are a type of machine learning model inspired by the structure and function of the human brain. These networks are made up of layers of artificial neurons, with each neuron receiving, processing, and transmitting information. Neural networks are trained using large volumes of data, and they adjust their internal connections (known as weights) to recognize patterns and make predictions. Deep neural networks – those composed of many interconnected layers – have driven significant advancements in AI by enabling machines to learn sophisticated and abstract representations of data.

Natural Language Processing (NLP)

Natural Language Processing refers to a machine's ability to understand and generate human language. This technology allows computers to interact with people using natural language, whether through text or voice. Virtual assistants like Siri, Alexa, and Google Assistant are examples of systems that use NLP to understand and respond to user queries.

This is the area that the media often highlights due to its potential to revolutionize information, communication, and the creation of all kinds of multimedia content. Natural Language Processing enables us to interact with computers as if they were one of us.

Large Language Models (LLMs)

Natural language processing combines with *Large Language Models* (LLMs) to revolutionize how machines interact with human language. LLMs – such as those developed in advanced models like GPT (*Generative Pretrained Transformer*) – take this process a step further by using vast datasets and deep neural networks to generate responses that are both sophisticated and contextually relevant.

These advancements have enabled major breakthroughs in fields like virtual assistants, automated content creation, and personalized digital interactions, transforming how individuals and organizations use technology to communicate and manage information.

These language models offer tremendous opportunities for ministry because of their accessibility and ease of use – no programming or technical background is needed to engage with them effectively.

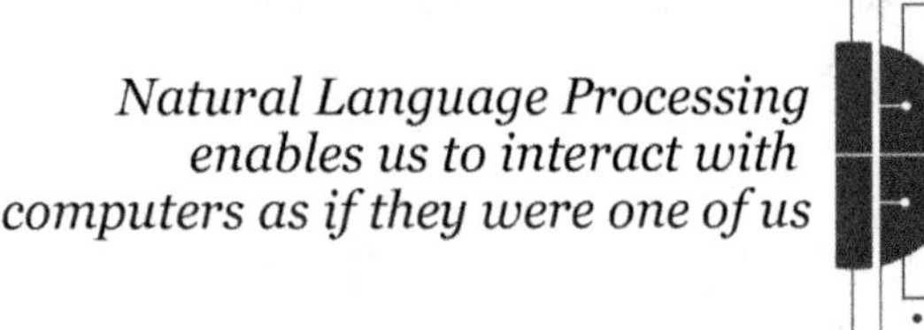

Data Science

Artificial intelligence relies heavily on data science to extract valuable insights from large volumes of information through a variety of models:

- Clustering models group similar data points together, making it easier to identify patterns or segments within a dataset.
- Classification models are used to assign categories to new data based on previously labeled examples.
- Predictive models anticipate future outcomes based on historical data.
- Recognition models, including pattern and object recognition, train systems to identify and classify elements in visual, textual, or auditory data.
- Decision trees are branching structures that help break down complex decisions into a series of simpler choices, providing clarity for automated decision-making.

All these models work together, leveraging data science to power AI algorithms and improve their accuracy and effectiveness.

Robotics

It's been a long time since Hero of Alexandria built his mechanical and pneumatic automata, but his ideas continue to inspire collective innovation, extending far beyond science fiction and popular culture.

Robotics uses machine learning and natural language processing to enhance AI performance in complex, precise physical tasks. In addition, computer vision enables machines to interpret images, videos, and sensory data from the real world. These technologies are key in fields such as industrial automation and autonomous vehicle navigation.

Video Games

Artificial intelligence plays a crucial role in creating dynamic and immersive gaming experiences. It is used to design complex behaviors in *non-playable characters* (NPCs), allowing them to react realistically to player actions, adapt to changing situations, and present intelligent challenges.

Moreover, AI can generate procedural content – such as entire levels or worlds – that adjusts automatically to the player's style, maintaining interest and variety. It is also applied to optimize game performance, adjusting difficulty in real time to balance the player experience and ensure the game is engaging but not frustrating. In this way, AI enriches gameplay and expands the creative possibilities for developers, enabling increasingly complex and compelling gaming experiences.

You can see how these layers of artificial intelligence relate to one another in Figure 1 on the next page.

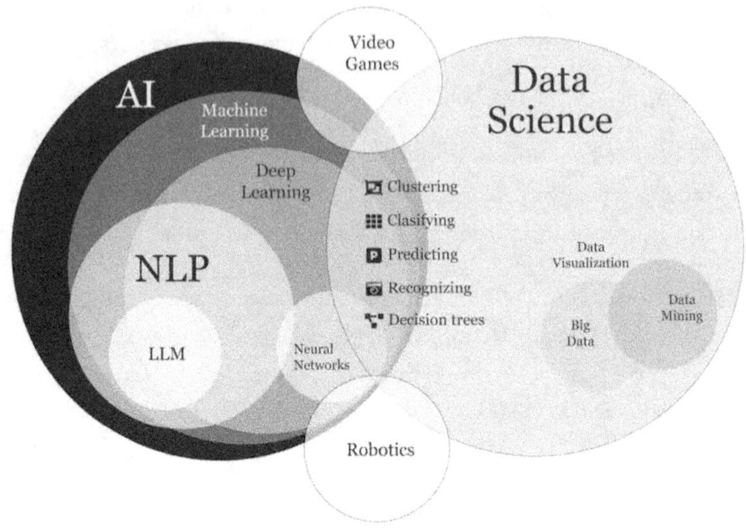

Figure 1: Artificial Intelligence Layers

Narrow AI vs. Strong AI

It is important to highlight that artificial intelligence is commonly divided into two categories: Narrow AI and Strong AI. Narrow AI refers to systems designed to perform specific tasks – such as playing chess or translating languages – without possessing true understanding or consciousness. Strong AI, on the other hand, is a more theoretical concept that refers to systems with cognitive capabilities including consciousness, self-awareness, and the ability to reason across a wide range of tasks.

Today, much attention is focused on the possibility of developing Artificial General Intelligence (AGI) – a form of strong AI with the capacity to perform any cognitive task at a level equal to that of human beings. Unlike narrow AI, which is designed for specific functions, AGI would be capable of learning, reasoning, and applying knowledge across a broad variety of contexts, demonstrating real understanding and adaptability.

This leads us to the relationship between AGI and Singularity. Singularity is a hypothetical point in the future when the development of AGI would trigger an exponential growth in superintelligent technology – intelligence that surpasses that of humans – producing unpredictable changes in society. Some theorists suggest that once we reach this point, AGI could begin improving itself without human intervention, potentially leading to a radical transformation of the world as we know it, with profound implications – both positive and negative – for humanity.

It is the topic of AGI that often sparks strong ethical and moral reactions, generating a variety of potential future scenarios. I will not delve deeply into these here, but cosmologist Max Tegmark explores them in depth in his book *Life 3.0: Being Human in the Age of Artificial Intelligence.* [3]

AI and Society

The current state of artificial intelligence reflects a period of rapid advancement and significant penetration across various areas of society. AI, which began as a theoretical discipline in the 1950s and 1960s, has evolved into a key technology in the digital age, with applications ranging from industrial automation to personalized medicine.

Today, AI not only enhances the efficiency of traditional processes but is also redefining what is possible across multiple domains.

Smart Applications

Applications such as virtual assistants on mobile devices and recommendation systems on streaming platforms have brought artificial intelligence into the public sphere, making it an integral part of everyday life. Additionally, tools like social media filters and real-time translation apps have shown how AI can enhance and personalize the user experience in a direct and tangible way.

Healthcare Systems

In the field of medicine, AI is being used to improve the diagnosis and treatment of diseases. Advanced AI algorithms analyze large volumes of medical data, such as X-rays and MRI scans, to detect patterns that human eyes might have missed. This has led to breakthroughs in early detection of illnesses like cancer, where AI can identify anomalies with greater accuracy and speed.

Moreover, personalized medicine – which uses AI to tailor treatments to a patient's individual characteristics – is revolutionizing preventive care and health management.

Commerce and Economy

In commerce and the economy, AI is driving a significant transformation. Profiling and recommendation systems, powered by machine learning algorithms, personalize the user experience on e-commerce platforms like Amazon and Netflix. These systems analyze user behavior and suggest products or content based on likely interests, thereby improving customer satisfaction and increasing sales.

In the financial sector, banks and other financial institutions use AI for risk analysis, fraud detection, and algorithmic trading, where investment decisions are made in fractions of a second based on real-time data.

Industrial Automation

AI has radically transformed industrial automation as well. In modern factories, AI-powered robots not only perform repetitive tasks but can also adapt to changing environments and work collaboratively with humans. This has led to greater efficiency, reduced errors, and increased flexibility in production. Supply chain management applications use AI to optimize inventory, logistics, and global product distribution.

Transportation

In transportation, AI is at the core of developments in autonomous vehicles. Companies like Tesla, Waymo, and Uber are heavily investing in creating self-driving cars that can operate safely without human intervention. These vehicles use a combination of sensors, cameras, and AI algorithms to make real-time decisions, such as avoiding obstacles, obeying traffic signals, and responding to changing road conditions. While fully autonomous vehicles are not yet common, advancements in this area are poised to transform urban mobility in the coming years.

Security

AI is being used in security and surveillance, enabling the monitoring of large geographic areas with drones, identifying suspicious behavior, and helping to prevent crimes. AI-enabled security cameras can analyze the flow of people in real time and alert authorities when unusual activity is detected. The military sector is also integrating AI into defense systems and autonomous weapons, sparking ethical debates over the role of AI in warfare.

Despite these advances, the current state of AI presents serious challenges. Data privacy, algorithmic bias, and ethical accountability are growing concerns as AI becomes increasingly embedded in daily life. The massive data collection required to train AI models poses risks to individual privacy, and the possibility that algorithms may replicate or amplify existing biases is a critical issue that must be urgently addressed.

Furthermore, the question of responsibility for decisions made by AI systems – especially in high-stakes contexts like healthcare or criminal justice – remains a topic of intense debate.

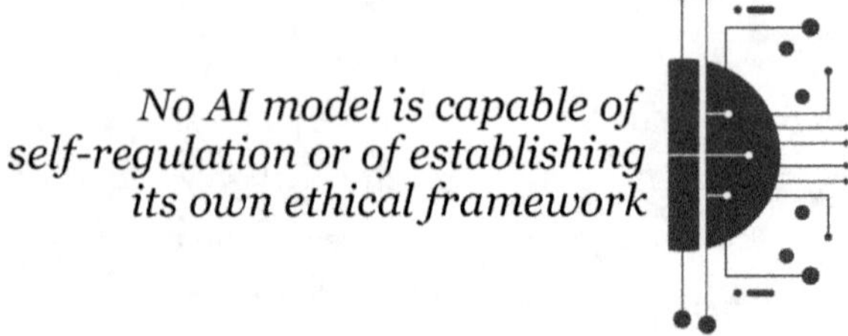

To conclude this brief introduction, artificial intelligence is currently at a pivotal point in its development. We now have applications that are transforming key sectors of society, with the potential to significantly improve people's lives. Yet, we have not established a broad ethical consensus to ensure its responsible use – one that guarantees equitable distribution of its benefits while minimizing the risks associated with its deployment.

No AI model is capable of self-regulation or of establishing its own ethical framework. This is precisely where the church, with its long-standing moral and ethical tradition and its foundational principles of freedom, purpose, and the sanctity of life, can step in to contribute meaningfully to the broader conversation – for the good of the ministry and of humanity, in alignment with theological truths and the church's cosmic mission.

Rather than withdrawing from the public discourse on artificial intelligence, this is a time for active presence and meaningful participation. Let us now take a closer look at the role of the church in the digital age.

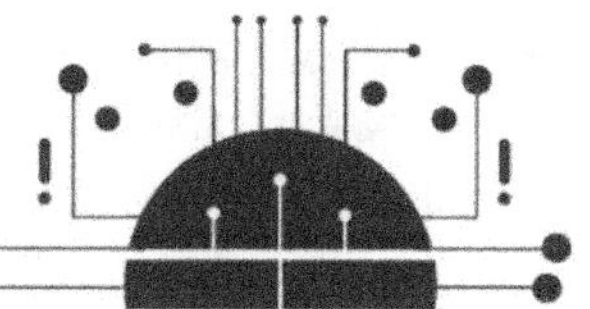

THE CHURCH IN THE DIGITAL AGE

We cannot afford to unreflectively muddle through the digital age. [4]

– JONAS KURLBERG, ENGLISH THEOLOGIAN.

I stand at the entrance of a world of unknown paths and interwoven walls. With each step, I move closer to my reward – but soon, I hit an obstacle. I bump into a wall, retreat, and learn from the mistake so I do not repeat it. I turn, move forward again, only to face another dead end. But I persist. Every failure brings me closer to my goal. After several attempts, my circuits align, the paths become clearer, and I accelerate toward the finish: a magnetic piece of cheese. With every synthetic bite, I know I've accomplished the unthinkable – learned, adapted, and triumphed. I am Theseus.

Theseus, the mechanical mouse that helped launch the digital era, was born in the 1950s. With remarkable precision, it navigated a maze of magnets and relays, moving methodically through corridors until it found its final reward. This was no ordinary mouse – it was one of the earliest physical manifestations of a concept that would go on to change the world forever: artificial intelligence.

The creator of this mechanical marvel was Claude Shannon, an American electrical engineer and mathematician whose vision and brilliance would earn him the title of "father of the digital age."

Theseus wasn't just a curious experiment – it was a physical representation of logical thinking and the capacity of a machine to "learn" from its environment. Fascinated by the idea that machines could solve problems on their own, Shannon designed Theseus to navigate a maze using an electromagnetic relay system that recorded each movement. If the mouse hit a wall, it logged that data and avoided repeating the mistake on future attempts. Eventually, Theseus would find the cheese every time – demonstrating a rudimentary form of learning.

Shannon's work with Theseus reflected his deep belief that machines could perform tasks traditionally associated with human intelligence – a revolutionary idea for his time.

Claude Shannon is best known for his foundational work in information theory – a field he essentially created. In his groundbreaking 1948 paper, *A Mathematical Theory of Communication*, [5] Shannon laid the groundwork for digital communication and data storage. This work didn't just revolutionize telecommunications – it became the bedrock for modern computing and artificial intelligence.

Shannon's theory of information focused on how messages could be efficiently encoded, transmitted, and decoded – even over noisy channels. He introduced key concepts like the bit – the fundamental unit of information – and developed the idea of entropy as a measure of uncertainty in a communication system. His work proved that all types of information – text, sound, images, and video – could be represented and processed digitally.

This mathematical approach to communication, data manipulation, and decision-making led to the development of algorithms that enabled machines to process information and perform tasks autonomously, laying the theoretical foundation for intelligent machines.

Throughout his life, Shannon exhibited an insatiable curiosity and an unmatched ability to approach problems in ways few others could.

His interdisciplinary thinking – blending mathematics, engineering, and a dose of creativity – sparked innovations that transformed not only technology but society itself. Shannon was not just a brilliant scientist; he was a visionary who saw the potential of machines to enhance and expand human capability.

The Digital Era

The Digital Age is a term used to describe the recent period in history during which digital technology has become central to society. This era began with the computer revolution in the second half of the 20th century and has expanded with the advent of the Internet, the proliferation of mobile devices, and the development of advanced technologies.

The word digital comes from the Latin *digitus*, meaning "finger." In a technological context, "digital" refers to the use of numbers – especially binary digits that represent electrical signals (0 for off and 1 for on) – to reduce information into a mathematical format, as proposed by Shannon. In a literal sense, it's a return to the technique of counting with one's fingers.

Unlike earlier eras dominated by analog and mechanical technologies, the digital age is defined by the ability to process, store, and transmit information at high speeds in digital form – transforming nearly every aspect of human life in profound ways.

Communication

The digital age has revolutionized the way we communicate. Email, social media, and instant messaging apps have made communication faster, more efficient, and global. Geographical barriers have faded, allowing people to stay connected with friends, family, and colleagues from anywhere in the world.

Digital platforms have also made it easier to form online communities where people share interests, opinions, and common causes – reshaping the dynamics of interpersonal relationships and social activism.

Economy

Digital transformation has had a profound impact on the global economy. E-commerce has fundamentally changed how we buy and sell goods and services. Companies like Amazon and Alibaba have reshaped the retail landscape, while platforms like Uber and Airbnb have fueled the rise of the sharing economy, where ownership is often replaced by access.

Digital finance – including cryptocurrencies and online banking – has redefined the concept of money and financial transactions, making them faster, more secure, and more globally accessible.

Education

Digitization has also transformed the field of education. With the rise of online learning platforms such as Coursera, Khan Academy, and edX, access to education has been democratized. Today, anyone with an internet connection can take courses from world-renowned institutions, no matter where they live.

In recent years, artificial intelligence has begun to personalize learning by adapting content and pacing to the unique needs of each student. This transformation has made education more inclusive and flexible, integrating learning more seamlessly into everyday life.

Healthcare

In healthcare, the digital age has driven significant advancements in prevention, diagnosis, and treatment. Telemedicine has made it possible for patients to receive care remotely, eliminating geographic barriers and increasing access to medical services in rural or underserved areas.

Electronic medical records and big data analytics have improved public health management, allowing faster and more effective responses to emergencies. Artificial intelligence is helping identify patterns in medical data that lead to more accurate diagnoses and personalized treatments – and it's also powering robotic innovations for remote surgeries.

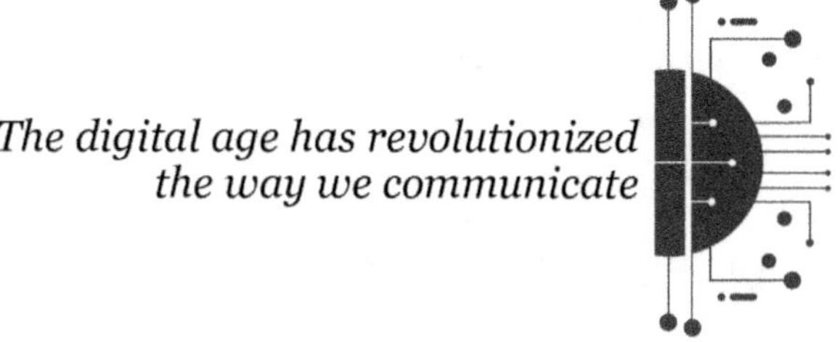

Entertainment

The digital age has completely reshaped the entertainment industry. Music, film, and video games have become on-demand, interactive experiences accessible on any internet-connected device. Streaming platforms like Spotify and YouTube have changed the way we consume content, offering nearly unlimited access to media anytime, anywhere.

Digital content creation has also been democratized. Anyone can now produce and share content with a global audience, radically changing the balance of power in the traditional entertainment industry.

Church

In this era of digital transformation, the Church is no exception. The digital age offers unprecedented opportunities to expand our reach, deepen our faith, and adapt our practices to meet contemporary needs. With digital tools, churches can connect with their congregations beyond physical limits through livestreams, mobile apps, and social media – making messages more accessible and spiritual resources easier to find. This shift accelerated during the COVID-19 pandemic.

Digital evangelism is another area with transformative potential. Through digital tools, we now reach global audiences, overcoming geographical and cultural barriers. Sermons, Bible studies, and educational resources can be distributed online, reaching people who might otherwise never access our faith communities.

Innovation in Tradition

In a world where technology is advancing at a dizzying pace, the Church faces the challenge of integrating digital innovations without losing sight of its centuries-old mission and central message. This adaptation is not only necessary for remaining relevant in today's society, but also for effectively fulfilling its role as a spiritual guide in an increasingly interconnected environment.

As we've seen, the digital age has transformed nearly every aspect of daily life – including the life of the Church. However, integrating digital technology into church life must be approached with balance, ensuring that our timeless traditions and doctrines are respected and preserved.

The digital age offers us unprecedented opportunities to expand our outreach, deepen our faith, and adapt our practices to our contemporary needs.

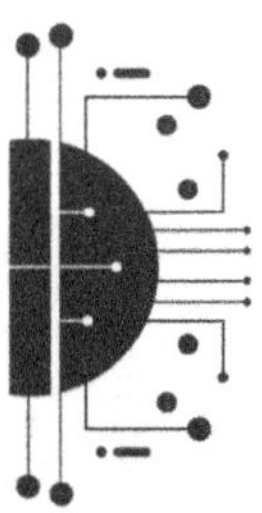

In Titus 2:1, Paul exhorts Titus, saying: "But as for you, speak the things which are fitting for sound doctrine." In the context of the Church's adaptation to the digital era, these words highlight the importance of maintaining the integrity of the Christian message while adopting new technologies. Though the Church may use digital tools to expand its reach and modernize its practices, every innovation must align with sound doctrine. Technology should be a means to faithfully communicate the Gospel – never compromising truth or diluting the core message of the Christian faith. In an increasingly digital world, the Church must continue to proclaim the solid teachings that have been its foundation throughout history, with clarity and conviction.

Innovation should not be seen as a threat but as a tool to reinforce and revitalize the fundamental values of Christianity. The key is to use technology in ways that serve the Church's mission without compromising its central message.

This is where the model of ministerial technologies I have developed in Books 1 and 2 of the *Cyberministry Series* comes into play. If you have not read them, I encourage you to do so – they present a framework for organizing technology strategically around the mission, along with a maturity model that leads us toward purposeful innovation.

One of the biggest challenges to faith in the digital era is preserving the practices of worship and liturgy, and the sense and solemnity of the sacraments, in a digital context. For example, livestreaming church services allows believers to participate from home, but it is essential that the virtual experience preserves reverence and devotion – something that can be difficult to achieve in a home environment. The Church must find ways to ensure these digital experiences are just as respectful and meaningful as those held in person.

Likewise, the Church can use technology to enrich its teaching without losing the depth of its doctrine. Online sermons and Bible studies offer a powerful opportunity to reach a wider audience, but they must retain theological rigor and faithfulness to the biblical message. While there is some ongoing work in this area, more remains to be done.

Another crucial aspect is how technology affects community within the Church. Social media and digital communication platforms can strengthen relationships among church members, allowing them to stay connected and support one another even when they cannot gather physically. However, it is vital that this digital connection does not replace face-to-face interactions, which are essential for building a strong and vibrant community.

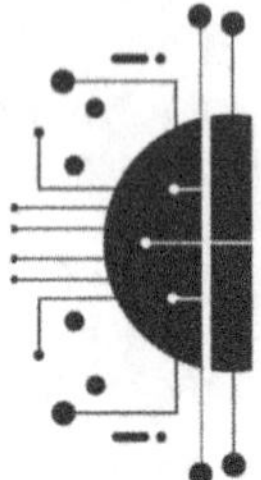

The Church can use technology to enrich its teaching without losing the depth of its doctrine

The Church must also be mindful of the ethical challenges posed by the digital age. The use of artificial intelligence, for example, offers new ways to personalize experiences and improve church administration. Yet the Church must also address issues such as data privacy, responsible technology use, and the risk of dehumanization – ensuring that digital tools are used ethically and in alignment with Christian values. I also address how the Church can develop foundational policies for technology use in my previously mentioned books.

Ministerial Technologies

In the first book of the *Cyberministry Series*, I explain the need to develop a new model to help churches think through, organize, plan, and manage technology with ministerial purposes in mind. This model takes a proactive, rather than reactive, leadership stance toward all forms of technology. It also emphasizes a pragmatic approach to technology, which leads us to the following definition of ministerial technologies:

> Ministerial technologies are an interconnected cultural network of people, systems, processes, policies, and devices that enable the church to fulfill the five essential functions of its mission in the world. [6]

Each of the five components in this definition of technology is placed in service of each of the five essential functions of the church's mission. I represent this relationship by the matrix in **Figure 2**.

This matrix is a practical tool. It is designed to help determine the role each of the five components of technology will play in each of the essential functions of your ministry. I encourage you to visit the Cyberministry website (https://cyberministry.info) to download a printable version of the matrix and use it as a discussion guide with your ministry team.

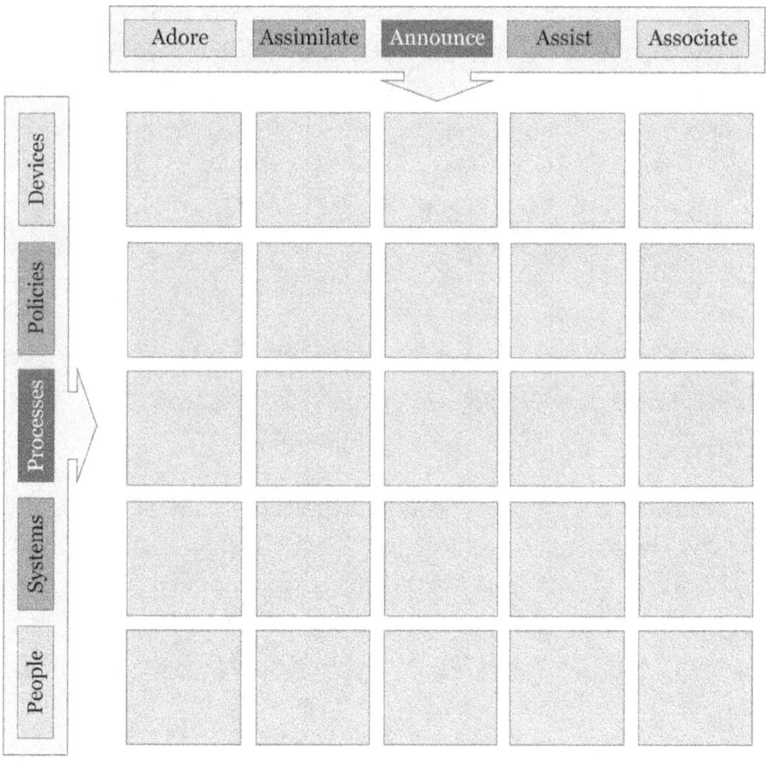

Figure 2: Ministerial Technologies Matrix®

I do not have time to go into all the details – for that, you can consult the book – but I will use the concept of ministerial technologies as a framework to develop the five aspects of a cyber-intelligent mission, since artificial intelligence can help us carry out the five core functions of the church's mission as expressed in the matrix: worship, learn, reach, help, and accompany.

This may seem to contrast with the current perception of AI within the church. In a 2024 survey conducted by Exponential, titled *State of AI in the Church 2024*, participants were asked: "*Which category of ministry work do you perceive as having the LEAST resistance to the integration of AI technologies?*"[7].

The results show that the areas with the least resistance were creative content production (34%) and administrative tasks (34%) – predictably, since these functions are viewed as logistical rather than spiritual. However, what stands out most is the low openness in areas that directly touch the core of pastoral ministry:

- Worship and sermon preparation (4%)
- Evangelism and outreach (4%)
- Pastoral care and counseling (3%)
- Christian education and discipleship (1%)
- Children's, youth, and senior ministry (1%)

Four of the core mission areas I explore in this book through the lens of cyberintelligence – worship, evangelism, spiritual formation, and community care – are at the very bottom of the list. This low openness reveals a deep cultural and theological resistance to integrating emerging tools into areas historically regarded as "sacred" or inherently human.

That mindset needs to change. Not because AI is the future of the church – God's mission does not depend on any particular tool – but because the church is called to discern the times and use every available resource wisely. To resist out of fear or unfamiliarity would be like the unfaithful servant who buried what his master entrusted to him: it limits our creativity, reach, and the impact of our witness. Just as the printing press served the Reformation and radio served the missionary movements, AI – when wisely integrated – can serve formation, worship, pastoral care, and proclamation.

The challenge is not to replace the ministry with machines, but to equip leaders to use AI as a faithful and ethical extension of their calling. This is an urgent invitation to renew our mindsets so that we do not get stuck in past methods but move forward with discernment into a cyberintelligent mission.

The church is in a unique position to embrace the opportunities of the digital age while preserving its ancient traditions. By integrating technology reflectively and carefully, the church can strengthen its mission to guide the faithful, expand its reach, and remain relevant in a rapidly changing world. The key is to find a balance – one that allows the church to innovate without losing its essence, using technology to serve spiritual and community purposes, all while upholding the timeless virtues of the Christian life: faith, hope, and love.

In was the Beginning the Word

The apostle John is known for the uniquely distinctive way he begins the narrative of his gospel. Before anything was, before anything that exists came into being – before all that is visible and invisible – there was the Logos. The Logos was the initiator of all things, the igniter of light, the opener of space, the giver of impulse, the spark that set every motion into play. The stopwatch of the ages.

Logos, translated as the Word, has intent and agency; it was the primary cause. Everything that exists, exists through Him, and without Him, nothing that has been made would have ever come into being.

> In the beginning was the Word, and the Word was with God, and the Word was God. He was in the beginning with God. All things were made through Him, and without Him nothing was made that was made. In Him was life, and the life was the light of men. And the light shines in the darkness, and the darkness did not comprehend it. (John 1:1-5).

This passage has always drawn me in with its depth and practicality. Stephen Covey used to say – and he also wrote: "all things are created twice. There's a mental or first creation, and a physical or second creation to all things"[8] I like to correct that by saying: all things are created three times. First, there's a mental creation, then a verbal one, and only then a physical creation.

Between the mind and reality, there is always the word. Think about it for a moment. An idea of a chair doesn't become a chair unless its design is first expressed in words – through sketches, on paper. A book moves from idea to page through words – so if you're thinking of writing one, sit down and release the words. A piece of software goes from idea to reality – evidently – through programming language, whether it's C#, Node.js, or Java.

And this idea extends far beyond that. A son or daughter becomes a person of character through the words planted in them by their parents. And what about our spiritual growth? We are transformed through the renewing of our mind by the living Word of God – "the light of humanity."

The theological affirmation of the centrality of the Logos, the divine Word, as the creative principle and means of revelation, has profound implications for the church's mission – especially in the context of the digital age. If from the beginning God revealed Himself through the Word, then communication is an essential part of the divine nature; our capacity for speech – which sets us apart from the rest of creation – is a vital part of our divine image; and our calling as a church to proclaim the Word to the world is central to our *raison d'être*.

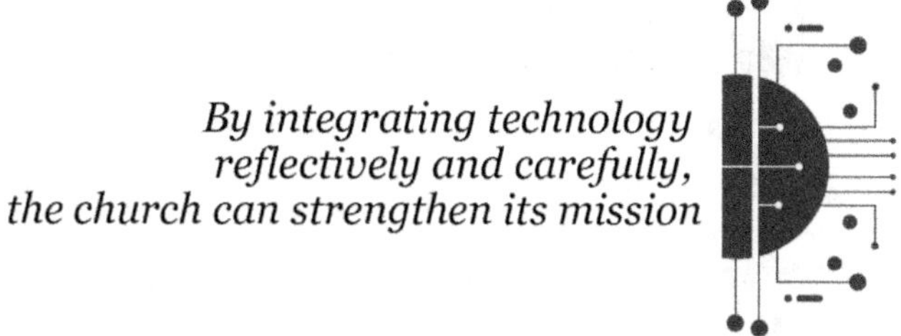

In this sense, technology has become a providential extension for continuing our communicative mission. Just as the incarnate Logos was how God made Himself known to humanity, today the church can use digital platforms as legitimate channels to proclaim the message of the Gospel with clarity, reach, and relevance. When used well, technological tools allow the Word to continue being heard "in the beginning" of this new era – crossing geographic, linguistic, and cultural borders without losing its essence or transformative power.

The church's mission remains the same, but its means have multiplied – and each one can serve as a faithful echo of the life-giving *Logos*.

Herein lies the power of natural language processing, as discussed in the introduction. The AI applications we have at our fingertips today function because of their ability to process language at speeds never seen in our technical development.

This is also why it's important to use words thoughtfully when interacting with language models. If you can articulate it clearly – and learn the techniques and patterns these models are trained to follow – artificial intelligence can help you bring it to life.

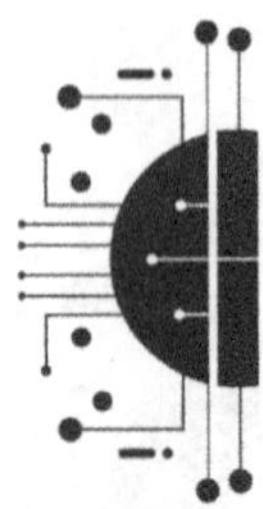

The church's mission remains the same, but its means have multiplied

Prompt Engineering

In this new landscape – where spoken and written words take digital form and interact with advanced language models – a vital skill emerges: prompt engineering.

This discipline, known as prompt engineering in English, involves the art of crafting requests, questions, or commands in a precise and strategic manner to interact effectively with artificial intelligence systems, particularly natural language processing models. Just as the Logos brought order to chaos with "Let there be light" – and there was – we too, when engaging with these technologies, must use language with clarity and purpose so that "let it be" becomes what we desire to build, analyze, or communicate. Artificial intelligence does not respond to the intention of the heart, but to the precision of our language.

From a spiritual and ministerial perspective, prompt engineering can be seen as a modern extension of the faithful use of words. Just as we preach, teach, and disciple with care, intention, and a biblical foundation, we must also learn to communicate with these new tools wisely. In fact, one of the byproducts of learning prompt engineering techniques is that we become better communicators ourselves.

It's not just about talking to a machine, it's about writing clearly what we want to be done, so that AI can collaborate with us in planning events, preparing sermons, translating messages, designing resources, or analyzing congregational data. A poorly crafted instruction can lead to vague or even counterproductive results, while a clear instruction can unlock creativity, efficiency, and pastoral depth.

That's why learning to formulate instructions with intelligence and purpose is, now more than ever, a ministerial competency. In this new stage of digital discipleship, every leader who desires to integrate technology into their mission must also become a kind of spiritual prompt engineer – someone who knows how to speak to the world, to their community, and now also to machines, with the same care that a good sower gives to the soil. Just as Paul prayed that his message would be clear for the edification of the church, our instructions to artificial intelligence should be crafted with precision, ethics, and ministry vision. After all, we are still called to proclaim the Word – even if now we do it from a keyboard or voice command – with the same spirit and the same truth.

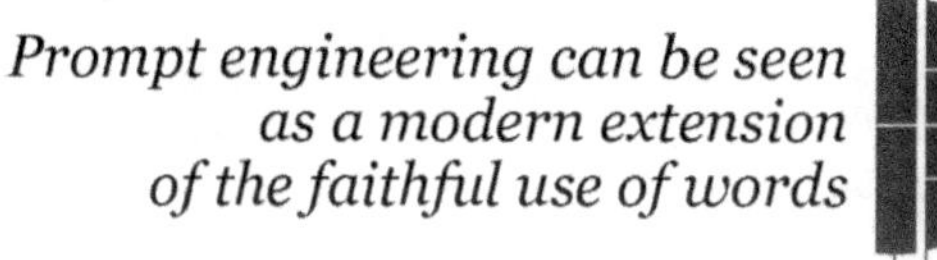

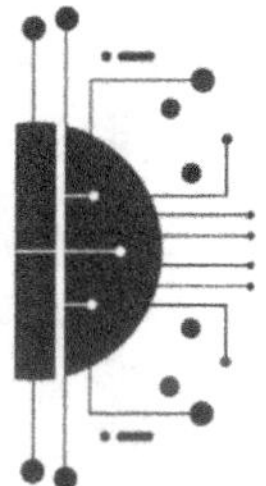

The DICTS Model

In our Inteliagentes training program, we use an interaction framework for working with artificial intelligence that we call DICTS – an acronym that helps anyone, especially ministry leaders, craft useful and consistent instructions for language models. Each letter represents a key action:

Dissect: Break down the purpose into smaller parts before writing the prompt.

Iterate: Try again. AI learns through the accumulated interaction history.

Contextualize: Provide data, tone, or prior information that the AI will use throughout the conversation.

Test: Change the approach or pattern if the result is not what you expected.

Structure: Write your prompt according to one of the templates that the system best understands.

This model helps reduce frustration, improves the quality of responses, and fosters a more strategic relationship between the leader and the tool. I encourage you to memorize it and keep it in mind always. To help with that, I offer it here as **Figure 3**.

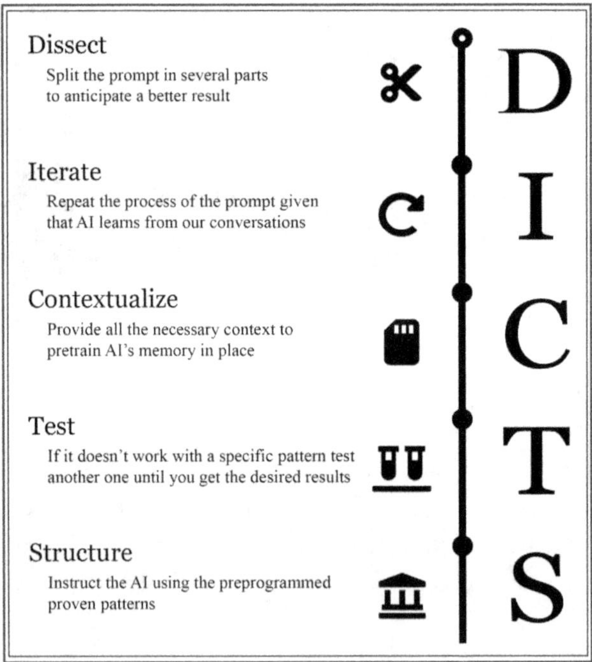

Figure 4: The DICTS Model

In the following chapters, I want to share with you some basic prompts that can help you become a spiritual prompt engineer – someone with the ability to deliver missional commands to artificial intelligence models in service of ministry goals. Use the DICTS model in your interactions with your preferred AI platforms.

These suggested prompts will appear like this:

> *"Act as an evangelical theologian in the style of Timothy Keller and analyze the relationship between innovation and tradition."*

And you can use them across various AI chat tools. Check the section on **AI Applications** for more details.

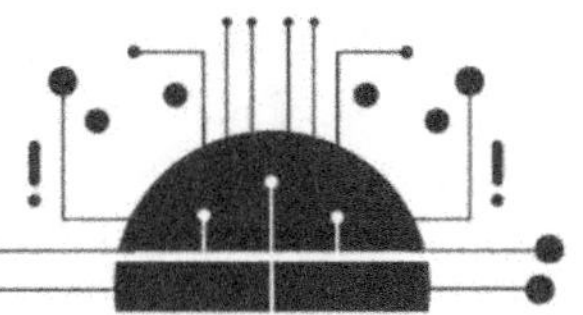

CYBERINTELLIGENT ADORING

A church that doesn't worship,
doesn't take care of its mission.

– A. W. TOZER, AMERICAN THEOLOGIAN AND AUTHOR.

We can use the instrument of technology to make much of God or we can use technology to our own means as a way to indulge our impulses and exalt ourselves. [9]

– AMANDA JENKINS, THEOLOGY PROFESSOR.

A heated exchange shattered the dense silence of the secluded Benedictine monastery. One phrase trampled over the next, like wild horses on the racetrack of ideas, racing to reach truth first. It was uncommon for voices to be raised in that place of prayer and contemplation, but that afternoon, tension overcame decorum:

– "Since when does the soul need instructions to sing?"

– "Since we forgot what truth sounds like – and now every community sings a different version."

– "Singing is divine! It can't be confined to lines and marks as if it were merchandise."

– "Inspiration doesn't die when written. On the contrary – it lives beyond us. And it cannot be preserved unless it is transmitted with precision."

The young monk took a deep breath, holding back frustration and gripping his parchment with resolve. He knew his proposals were unsettling his brothers. In the chapel, singing was a living tradition, passed down by ear and memory. To change that felt, to many, like desecrating the sacred.

He was no rebel. He was a seeker. He watched with sadness how Gregorian chant – this jewel of the soul – was increasingly fragmented with every visit to another monastery. What was meant to unify the Church in prayer had become a melodic Tower of Babel. How could one preserve the purity of sacred chant without relying on fragile human memory?

The answer came in lines. First one, then two, and eventually four. Upon them, dots, marks, and letters: a codification of what once floated freely – and thus, soon to perish. This was the birth of musical notation.

The monk's name was Guido of Arezzo, who lived in the 11th century in the Abbey of Pomposa, on the Adriatic coast near Ferrara, Italy. He developed a system of musical writing that would allow novices to learn chant in weeks instead of years. His invention gave rise to what we now know as the staff, and with it, a new era of sacred music began.

Before Guido, liturgical chants were transmitted orally. Each community had its own versions, and many were lost with the death of the lead cantor. Learning was slow, confusing, and dependent on constant repetition. Guido saw writing not as a betrayal of the Spirit, but as a service to unity and faithful transmission.

But not everyone saw it that way.

Many feared that notation would kill spontaneity, that it would turn expression rigid – that monks would sing while staring at lines instead of lifting their souls to God. Would this not be granting more power to technique than to devotion? Was there not a risk of turning worship into mechanical routine?

Valid objections. Real concerns. And yet, as with any meaningful technology, time proved that the new had not come to destroy, but to preserve, expand, and enrich. Thanks to notation, sacred chants could travel across Europe, span generations, and harmonize voices separated by distance and language. Tradition wasn't replaced, but faithfully transmitted and clarified.

Today, a thousand years later, we face a similar dilemma.

Artificial intelligence has entered our lives – even our churches. Some receive it with excitement, others with caution, and still others with outright rejection.

"Won't AI make worship impersonal?"

"Will we become dependent on algorithms instead of the inspiration of the Holy Spirit?"

"Aren't we risking losing the human in the divine?"

The questions sound strikingly familiar – echoes of Guido's time.

And, as then, the answer lies not in fearing the tool, but in discerning its purpose. Just as the staff became an extension of the human ear and a register for posterity, AI can become an extension of our creativity, sensitivity, and spiritual vision – if used with wisdom and reverence – as a springboard into the future.

Worship is not the property of any one form, nor is it confined to any one medium. If, in the 11th century, a quill on parchment extended the soul's song, then in the 21st century, a digital server may well help us raise new songs, build new connections, and discover new ways to glorify the same God who is worthy forever and ever.

More than Sounds and Aesthetics

Before there were LED screens, digital mixers, or algorithms suggesting playlists, worship already resonated in the hearts of believers. Worship, in its purest essence, is not a collection of harmonious sounds or a well-produced aesthetic experience. It is the soul's response to the glory of God. It is the intentional act of recognizing who He is and placing ourselves humbly in our rightful position: creatures before the Creator, the redeemed before the Redeemer.

Throughout biblical history, worship is a constant expression of faith and surrender. In Exodus, we see Moses asking Pharaoh for freedom – not just to escape, but "so that they may worship Me in the wilderness" (Exodus 7:16). In the Psalms, worship comes through songs, laments, praise, dancing, and silence. (Wouldn't it be something if David – or one of the sons of Korah – had invented musical notation? We might know how the original tracks sounded!)

In the New Testament, Jesus declares that the Father seeks worshipers "in spirit and in truth" (John 4:23), emphasizing that worship is not bound by place or style, but by the authenticity of the heart.

In this light, any technology incorporated into worship must adhere to this principle: make room for God's presence, and answer the question: Does it lead the worshiper to greater awareness of that presence? Does it point to divine glory – or to human production?

We live in an era where visual and sonic production has become incredibly sophisticated. Well-programmed lights, finely mixed tracks, and dynamic visuals can create powerful experiences. But if the content of those experiences doesn't arise from an encounter with

God or point back to Him, we're crafting atmospheres – not transformation.

Technology can serve as a supportive instrument, but it cannot be the center. The center is Christ, and the goal is the glory of God. Every technological innovation must be evaluated through this lens – not by how impressive it sounds or looks, but by how faithfully it leads to a genuine experience of worship.

Worship is not for consumption – it is to offer it.

It is not to be impressed – it is to be transformed.

And for that, not even the most advanced artificial intelligence can replace a contrite heart seeking the Lord.

In this light, any technology incorporated into worship must adhere to this principle: make room for God's presence

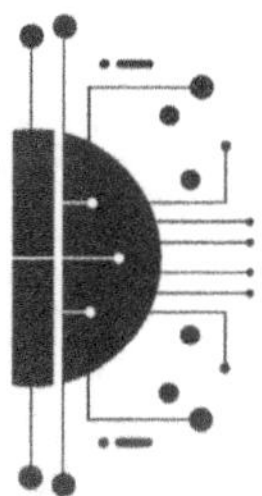

Altar Allies

At the heart of every Christian gathering lies the eternal call to exalt God. Worship is far more than a decorative moment or a transition – it is one of the deepest forms of encounter with the divine. In worship, the community is formed, truth is declared, and the soul is surrendered. In our generation, artificial intelligence (AI) does not replace this mystery, but it can become a powerful ally – facilitating the preparation, collaboration, and expression of that worship. As in the days of Guido of Arezzo, the tool must serve the spiritual purpose, not compete with it.

It is possible to integrate cyberintelligent worship in practical, strategic, and faithful ways that honor the heart of Christian devotion.

Each application rests on a fundamental premise: AI can assist – but never replace. It doesn't sing for us, it doesn't feel for us, but it can help us organize, amplify, and better communicate our collective worship.

Write Adapted Lyrics

One of the most exciting possibilities of AI in ministry is the composition of worship lyrics adapted to the specific message the church is teaching during a season. This practice, historically reserved for professional songwriters and musicians, can now be democratized and become collaborative.

Imagine the Sunday sermon theme is God's faithfulness in uncertainty. You can ask an AI model to generate lyrics that reflect that truth – drawing on specific Bible passages, expressing a particular emotional tone (hope, stillness, gratitude), and matching a musical style that fits your community's culture. The key is to use the tool not as a replacement for inspiration, but as a spark – one that creative ministers can adapt, revise, and make their own.

> *Write lyrics for a congregational worship song based on Lamentations 3:22–23 and Hebrews 10:23. The theme is God's faithfulness in times of doubt. It should have a hopeful tone and suit a soft, repetitive, easy-to-sing melody."*

Automated Song Curation

Another useful application is curating song lists. You no longer must manually sift through hundreds of songs to find one that aligns with the day's teaching. AI can suggest themed playlists based on a sermon topic, liturgical series, or even a single spiritual focus word. It can also consider vocal ranges, musical preferences, and available instruments.

This doesn't eliminate pastoral discernment – it enhances it with efficiency. Rather than improving at the last minute, planning becomes more intentional and theologically precise.

> *Suggest five contemporary worship songs for a multigenerational congregation. This week's message is 'God is our Rock.' Include songs focused on security, trust, and God Almighty's strength."*

Score Generation and Vocal Arrangements

AI can also generate sheet music and vocal arrangements tailored to the skill levels in a worship team. This includes simplifying melodies for beginners or creating harmonies for full vocal teams. It can even turn a basic MIDI file or a simple recording into a formatted score.

This not only saves time – it empowers more people to participate musically, regardless of experience.

> *"Create a lead sheet in C major for a simple congregational worship song, with vocal arrangements for soprano, alto, and tenor. The lyrics focus on God's peace in the midst of the storm."*

AI-Assisted Music Production

AI can also generate sheet music and vocal arrangements tailored to the skill levels in a worship team. This includes simplifying melodies for beginners or creating harmonies for full vocal teams. It can even turn a basic MIDI file or a simple recording into a formatted score.

This not only saves time – it empowers more people to participate musically, regardless of experience.

> *"Suggest a chord progression and minimal instrumentation for a slow worship song in A minor with a contemplative and reverent tone"*

Live Translation & Subtitling

For multicultural congregations, language can be a worship barrier. AI can now provide real-time translation of lyrics, slides, and sermons – generating automatic subtitles during live services. This allows everyone to sing the same song – even in different languages – creating a unified and deeply inclusive experience.

> *"Translate these worship lyrics from Spanish to English while keeping the meter and poetic tone: 'Tú eres fiel, Señor, cada mañana renuevas tu amor."*

Real-Time Visuals

AI can also integrate with visual systems to produce adaptive stage visuals, graphic transitions, and atmospheric projection based on song lyrics or service flow. This doesn't replace the Holy Spirit – but it can help focus attention and create a worshipful environment.

For example, if the song is about creation, the system can project nature scenes. If the theme is the fire of the Spirit, it might project warm textures or stylized flames – all synchronized with the worship experience.

> *"Generate a slow, gentle visual sequence representing the peace of God to be projected during a worship song about resting in the Lord. Include blue and green tones, without distracting elements."*

These tools alone do not make worship more spiritual. The Spirit does not dwell in technology – but in surrendered hearts. But when used with discernment and pastoral vision, these technologies can:

- Broaden congregational participation
- Reduce technical burdens on leaders
- Foster excellence without elitism
- Boost creativity with spiritual focus
- Include those previously excluded due to language, ability, or resources

The key is not what AI can do on its own, but what it can enable when placed in the hands of a worshiping community – one that leads with heart, mind, and hands. AI doesn't replace inspiration – but it can be part of the redemptive creative process.

AI doesn't sing.

But it can help more people find their voice.

And when used wisely, that is not replaced worship – it is augmented worship.

Worship cannot be outsourced.

AI can suggest a melody, mix a track, or translate a lyric – but it cannot surrender in worship. It has no soul, no faith, no gratitude.

In the end, only the human worshiper is irreplaceable.

Spectators More Than Participants

In the enthusiasm to adopt new technologies, there is a risk of moving from wise assistance to unconscious dependence. Without clear theological discernment, automation in worship can slowly displace what is essential: the spiritual communion between God and His people.

One of the subtler dangers is the illusion of spiritual excellence. A perfectly produced service – with flawless music, immersive visuals, and synchronized execution – may seem "successful," even if it lacks authenticity in delivery. Worship runs the risk of becoming an aesthetic experience – emotionally satisfying but spiritually shallow – where performance is evaluated more than presence.

Moreover, excessive centralization on technical aspects can make the participation of the congregation invisible. When everything is automated – audio mixing, song selection, vocal harmonization – community members may feel more like spectators than participants. Opportunities to train new musicians, teach musical theology, and pastor emerging gifts with patience are reduced. Worship becomes a finished product, not an offering built in community.

There is also the risk of replacing spiritual preparation with quick fixes. Why meditate on the Word or seek inspiration in prayer if a generative tool can write song lyrics in seconds? Convenience can feed spiritual laziness. A song composed by AI, without passing through the filter of the human soul, may sound right but lack anointing.

Finally, artificial intelligence may lead us to depend on the predictable. Biblical worship is full of spontaneous moments, divine interruptions, and unexpected responses. If everything is controlled by pre-programmed sequences or computer-generated responses, will we leave room for the movement of the Spirit?

For this reason, integrating AI into worship requires leadership with discernment. The problem is not using technology but using it without pastoral wisdom. What is gained in precision can be lost in depth if there is no spiritual vigilance. We must continually ask: does this facilitate worship or replace it? Does it bring us closer to the throne of God or just to the center of the stage?

With these risks in mind, the goal is not to avoid innovation, but to embrace it with open eyes and aligned hearts. As pastors, musicians, designers, and leaders, we must remember that we are not called to impress, but to guide the congregation in spirit and truth.

Augmented, Not Replaced, Worship

History has shown us that every technical advancement in the church – musical notation, the printing press, radio, video – brought new opportunities to proclaim the Gospel and build up the faith. Artificial intelligence is no different in its potential, but it does demand greater discernment due to its capacity to simulate, automate, and even "create" spiritual content.

To speak of augmented worship is not to imagine a futuristic service with robots in the pulpit, but to recognize that digital tools can enrich the worship experience when used wisely. To augment means to strengthen, enrich, expand – not to supplant.

AI can help us personalize experiences, include previously excluded people, plan with greater biblical and musical coherence. It can support overburdened leaders, train new teams more quickly, and reduce technical barriers so that worship flows with less friction.

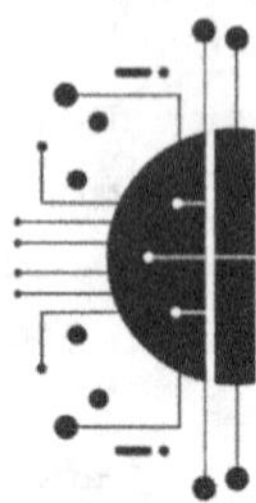

Integrating AI into worship requires leadership with discernment

But the heart of worship remains human and spiritual. Confession, prayer, congregational singing, proclamation of the Word, and the Lord's Supper cannot be reduced to data streams. They are sacred acts that require presence, community, and discernment.

Therefore, in adopting cyber-intelligent worship, the goal should not be to make worship "easier" but more faithful. Not faster, but deeper. Not more spectacular, but truer. At this stage in the church's history, AI can be an ally – but it should not be a leading voice at the altar. That still belongs to the Holy Spirit and to people willing to listen.

An Altar Without Artifice

Hero of Alexandria designed mechanisms that opened doors automatically, made statues speak, and poured offerings by themselves. All to create awe, so that the people would believe the gods were present. It was technology in the service of spectacle – not of truth.

But Christian worship is not born of manufactured wonder, but of real encounter with a living God. Our goal is not to impress, but to surrender. We do not seek to astonish people, but to lead them into a presence that transforms.

Artificial intelligence can assist us with songs, visuals, or translations, but fire does not fall on intelligent systems – it falls on surrendered hearts. The Christian altar does not need smoke or self-opening doors; it needs truth, humility, and Spirit.

The church that honors the Lord in this era will not be the most technologically advanced, but the most faithful in spirit and in truth. Let AI serve us, yes. But let it never take the place of the worshipper.

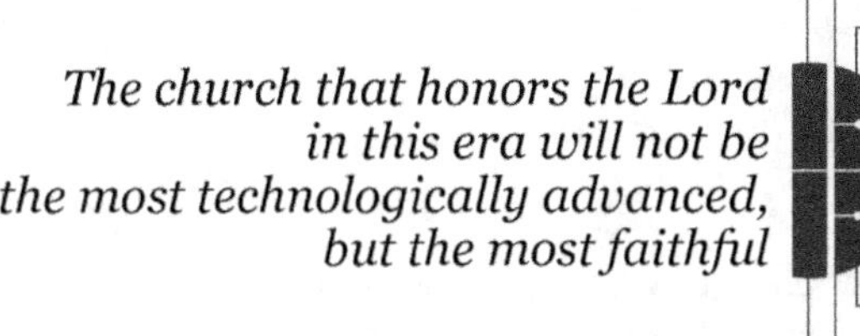

Let's now consider how artificial intelligence has the potential to facilitate learning and discipleship, but before that, here is a template prompt you can adapt to your liturgical style and congregational context:

"Act as a Christian worship director with pastoral experience in multicultural contexts and multigenerational congregations. Your approach combines theological sensitivity, liturgical planning, and a deep understanding of the worshiper's heart.

Help me plan a worship service for next Sunday. The central theme of the message will be 'God's faithfulness in the midst of uncertainty', based on Lamentations 3:22–23 and Hebrews 10:23.

Please suggest the following:

– Three congregational songs that reinforce this theme, including lyrics or thematic references.

– A call to worship to be read at the beginning of the service, no more than 100 words, based on the biblical texts.

– A brief transition prayer between the second and third song.

– A closing thought or verse to conclude the time of worship before the sermon.

The tone should be pastoral, reverent, and hopeful. The music should be accessible to a congregation diverse in age and cultural background."

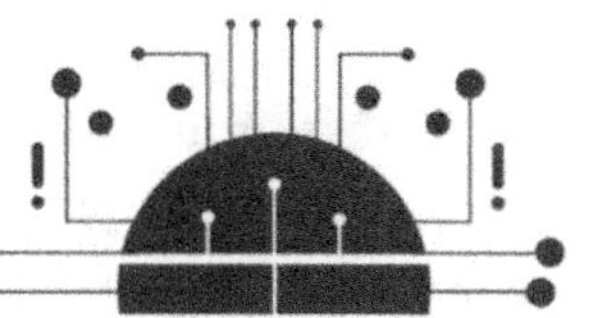

CYBERINTELLIGENT ASSIMILATING

By embracing innovative approaches that are relevant to their specific contexts in the digital age, churches can continue to develop and multiply disciples in the future. [10]

– DAVE BENSON, LAUSANNE MOVEMENT.

The Greeks learned in order to comprehend. The Hebrews learned in order to revere. The modern man learns in order to use. [11]

- ABRAHAM HESCHEL, POLISH RABBI.

My fingers smell of ink and wax. The morning light barely filters through the stone windows of the scriptorium in Wessobrunn, in my humble Bavarian village. Silence has already settled in as a sacred guest. A half-finished codex awaits me: the Latin Psalter I began weeks ago, with letters as tall as towers and illuminated initials adorned with gold leaf.

Copying the Scriptures is not merely a task of precision; it is an act of worship. Every stroke is a prayer. Every decorated margin is an offering. I do not sign my works, but sometimes they call me "the sister who writes as if she sings with her hand." That is enough for me. I do not need to be known, only faithful. God already sees me and knows my name. I am Diemoth.

As I work, I think of those who will read these centuries from now. Perhaps a novice who barely understands Latin, perhaps a preacher seeking comfort, perhaps someone wrestling with faith. For them, I repeat each line three times and mix my pigments with patience. I do not write to decorate the world, but to uphold it with truth.

Yet not everyone sees it that way. Some voices among the brothers say that such decoration is vanity. That simplifying the texts would be more practical. That beauty distracts. But I do not believe that order and light are enemies of truth. The same God who wove the heavens with stars gave us the desire to adorn what is sacred. The Psalm doesn't only sing because of what it says, but because of how it says it. Form also speaks. I think of this as I illuminate:

> The heavens declare the glory of God; And the firmament shows His handiwork (Psalms 19:1).

Sometimes I wonder if there might be a faster way to copy Scripture. A swifter hand, a more precise technique. But I always return to the same thought: what matters is not just the message, but the reverence with which it is transmitted. It's not only about letters, but about the attitude of the soul that writes them.

This story, as Netflix might say, is based on true events – but it was not written by Diemoth herself… though you guessed that already. This is my attempt to explore her mindset while engaged in one of the most treasured contributions in the history of church technology.

Today, centuries later, we no longer write on parchment with goose quills. Today, those who teach, preach, and translate sacred scriptures have new tools: screens, code, and of course, artificial intelligence. What once took months to copy is now produced in seconds. But the question raised in Wessobrunn still remains: how is truth transmitted faithfully?

Cyberintelligent learning presents the same spiritual challenge that medieval scriptoriums once faced: how to honor the eternal Word using the tools of the moment. Artificial intelligence allows us to study the Bible quickly, generate sermon outlines in minutes, translate complex texts with near-instant precision, and adapt content for different cultures, languages, and levels of understanding. Powerful tools. Fast. Brilliant. Enlightened.

But are they reverent?

The real challenge does not lie in the tool, but in the heart of the one who uses it. Just as Diemoth adorned each verse with intention and prayer, pastors, educators, and leaders today must learn to use artificial intelligence not to lighten their spiritual load, but to expand their faithfulness. They must seek not just efficiency, but depth. Not just reach, but integrity.

As then, beauty is still possible. Truth is still sacred. And though the form may change, the calling remains the same: to write the Word on the tablets of the heart, with ink, with light… or with data, if necessary.

And you – are you making the transition from handcrafted manuscripts to AI-powered knowledge engines?

Prepare Intelligently, Preach Wisely

Preaching is one of the most sacred acts in the life of the church. It's not about speaking well, but about speaking faithfully. Every time someone stands to proclaim the Scriptures before a congregation, what's at stake is not just the clarity of the message but the transformation of those who hear it.

For centuries, sermon preparation has been an artisanal process: prayer, Bible study, searching for illustrations, crafting outlines, revising language, and connecting with the life of the community. And it still is. But today, artificial intelligence can accompany this process with tools that multiply effectiveness without reducing depth, if the preacher maintains the spiritual center of the calling.

Some of these ideas I first shared in my article, *3 Failproof Patterns to Generate Your Sermon Outlines*, though what follows here is more complete.[12] I want to share several ways AI can support preaching.

Researcher with a Critical Eye

Responsible preaching requires more than inspiration – it demands careful research, source analysis, contrasting theological perspectives, and historical discernment. AI can act as a preliminary research assistant, especially useful when the preacher has limited time or needs to explore a topic from multiple angles.

For example, when preparing a series on the Kingdom of God, the preacher might ask the AI for an overview of historical interpretations (Augustinian, premillennial, "Kingdom now" theology), with relevant quotes, key differences, and pastoral applications. Such research might take hours with books and articles, but deep research models can offer an initial summary, which the preacher can verify, expand, and adapt with discernment.

This is key: AI does not replace the judgment of the researcher, but it can sharpen the focus. Like any good scribe, it helps gather, compare, and synthesize – without dictating conclusions. It's a flashlight in the library, not the librarian.

> *"Act as a theological researcher. Provide a comparative summary of Kingdom theology in Augustine of Hippo, George Eldon Ladd, and Dallas Willard. List at least three key differences, their impact on pastoral practice, and their relationship to eschatology."*

Exegesis Study Assistant

One of AI's most useful applications in preaching is textual and thematic analysis of biblical passages. A well-trained language model can help identify literary structures, keywords, parallels, cross-references, and even suggest relevant historical or patristic commentary. It does not replace Bible study but can speed it up and enrich it.

> *"Act as an evangelical theologian trained in biblical languages. Help me analyze Romans 8:1–11. Give me a summary of its structure, central message, and possible pastoral applications for a congregation struggling with guilt."*

Message Organizing Support

AI can also help organize sermon ideas. Sometimes the preacher has theological clarity but struggles with structure: Where to begin? How to connect the parts? What illustrations will reinforce the teaching? AI can act as an editorial assistant suggesting logical outlines, narrative models, or thematic approaches – always editable by the preacher.

> *"Help me outline a sermon on God's faithfulness, based on Lamentations 3:21–23. The message should have three main points, an introduction based on a true story, and a conclusion that calls the audience to hope."*

Relevant and Contextualized Illustrations

A challenge in modern preaching is finding relevant illustrations for a diverse audience. AI can suggest current examples, historical stories, cultural images, and metaphors tailored to the demographic of a given community.

> *"Suggest three modern illustrations to explain the difference between grace and merit for an urban audience aged 20–30."*

Clarity and Accessibility of Language

Many preachers have deep biblical understanding but struggle to translate it into everyday language. AI can help simplify discourse without diluting content – adjusting vocabulary, reducing jargon, or rewriting in a conversational tone.

> *"Rewrite this theological paragraph in clear language while maintaining doctrinal depth: 'Justification by faith implies an external imputation of righteousness based on the vicarious work of Christ."*

Multilingual and Multicultural Preaching

For churches with multilingual audiences or transitioning cultural contexts, AI can be a great ally in contextual sermon translation. It's not just about translating words, but adapting examples, imagery, and references to the listener's cultural framework.

> *"Translate this sermon outline from Spanish to English, adapting Latin cultural references to U.S. equivalents, while keeping a pastoral and biblical tone."*

What matters most is not how much AI can do, but how we use it as servants of the message – not as substitutes for the spiritual process. AI can help us organize, illustrate, and connect – but it can't replace conviction, prayer, or the discernment of the Holy Spirit.

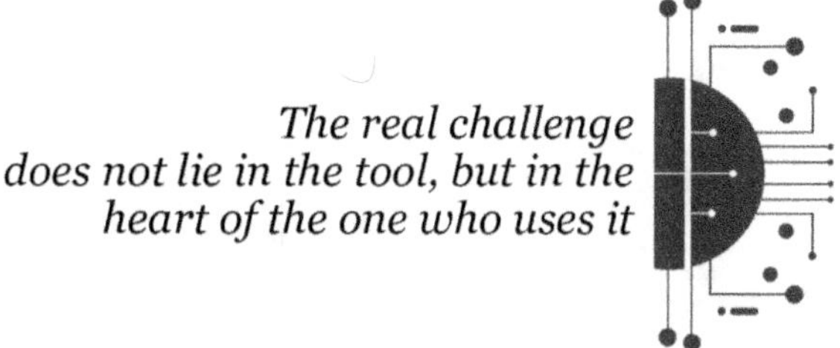

A sermon you create in just seconds may sound correct, but only a message born out of communion with God can touch the human heart. This is why using AI in preaching preparation does not mean you have to renounce your spiritual gifts but to respond to higher a responsibility: To us each resource within our reach to prepare the sermon with excellence and to proclaim its message with integrity.

Classrooms That Learn

Christian teaching has always been both communal and personal. Jesus didn't only teach crowds from a boat; He also walked with His disciples, answered questions, corrected with patience, and tailored His parables to the heart of each listener. That is the root of discipleship: teaching adapted to the soul.

Today, within the context of digital learning, this personalized vision can be enriched by the capabilities of artificial intelligence. We are no longer limited to "one-size-fits-all" materials created by a publishing machine in contexts likely foreign to our own.

With AI-powered educational platforms, it's now possible to offer formative experiences adaptable to the pace, level, style, and needs of each learner – something of incalculable value for ministry. With that in mind, I want to offer you three use cases in a pool of possibilities.

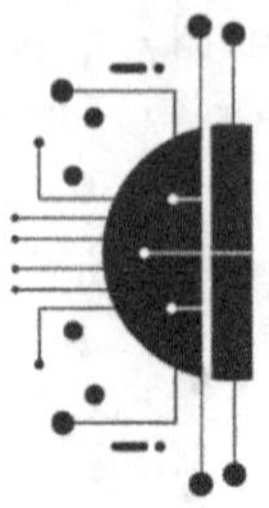

With AI-powered educational platforms, it's now possible to offer adaptable formative experiences

AI as a Digital Mentor

AI can serve as an accompanying tutor. It can summarize texts, pose questions, and suggest challenges based on the learner's progress. It can recommend related Bible verses, complementary resources, or application exercises tailored to the student's comprehension level or age. In contexts where human mentors are scarce, this technology does not replace the teacher, but it helps multiply their reach.

This has direct applications in:

- Sunday schools (adaptive materials by age or experience)
- Bible institutes (theological studies with automated feedback)
- Small groups (shared reading with customized guides and presentations)
- One-on-one discipleship (study plans tailored to the learner's spiritual maturity).

Prompt example:

> *"Act as a Christian mentor. Design a Bible reading and study plan for someone new to the faith, with emphasis on the character of God, grace, and following Jesus. Include weekly objectives, key verses, and reflection questions."*

Multimodal and Inclusive Learning

Many artificial intelligence platforms offer content in multiple formats: audio, text, video, interactive summaries. These are known as multimodal models. Think about it: you can now generate images, videos, presentations, or infographics from theological concepts.

This enables people with different learning styles – auditory, visual, kinesthetic – to engage meaningfully with biblical formation.

It's also an opportunity to break barriers: people with disabilities, low literacy, or from multicultural contexts can access quality teaching without feeling excluded. The Kingdom expands when learning adapts to the full diversity of the body of Christ.

Ongoing Leadership Development

AI is also facilitating continuous learning for pastors and leaders, using systems that identify theological, doctrinal, or ministerial growth areas, and recommend short modules for review, updates, or deeper learning. A rural pastor without access to seminaries can still receive solid, up-to-date training with the right digital support.

> *"Recommend a continuing education path for a small group leader with little formal Bible knowledge. Include materials on how to interpret the Bible, teach clearly, and provide spiritual care for others."*

Cyberintelligent learning does not aim to replace the teacher or mentor, but to extend their presence. Just as Jesus multiplied bread to feed thousands, today AI can multiply resources to form disciples – without compromising truth or relationship.

The goal is not to automate discipleship, but to strengthen it. Not to teach faster, but to form more deeply. Just as every medieval classroom was centered on the text and the teacher, today our digital classrooms must remain centered on Christ and His Word, no matter how sophisticated the tools become.

Dethroning Babel

In the story of Babel, humanity sought to reach the heavens by building a tower with its own ingenuity, using a single language to assert itself as its own god (Genesis 11:1–9).

But God confused their language, scattering them to stop a unity born of pride. In contrast, on the day of Pentecost, God restored understanding between languages – not through human effort, but through the Spirit (Acts 2:1–12). There we see that true unity does not come from mastering language, but from surrendering to the Word.

Today, in the digital age, we are tempted to use artificial intelligence to rebuild Babel: to multiply knowledge, centralize control, and standardize faith. But the call of the Kingdom is different. It's not about imposing one voice but serving each people group in their own language, culture, and path to truth. When we use AI to translate, explain, and contextualize Scripture, we are not exalting the human tower – we are tearing down its pride, making it possible for every tongue to confess Jesus as Lord, in their own language.

The translatability of the Gospel is one of the marvels of Christian history. From Aramaic to Greek, from Latin to the vernaculars, every generation has translated Scripture so that new peoples might know Christ. Translation, however, is no small task – it requires linguistic sensitivity, theological knowledge, and fidelity to the original text. And here, artificial intelligence is opening new possibilities.

Of course, not without its challenges. Translation by language models works far better in languages with a rich written heritage, and far less in oral languages or those with limited documentation. These models interpret based on the language they've been trained in.

Still, today's AI tools allow pastors, teachers, and students to compare Bible versions, translate sermons, and analyze keywords in Greek or Hebrew without requiring years of technical training. This democratizes advanced biblical study, making deeper understanding accessible to more people – not just experts.

Now let me expose some use cases.

Contextualized Translation for Diverse Communities

In many congregations today, more than one language is spoken, or members have a mother tongue different from that of the preacher. With AI, it's now possible to translate sermon outlines, lessons, or devotionals almost instantly – preserving not just meaning, but pastoral tone and doctrinal clarity.

More than literal translation, AI can help adapt cultural references, imagery, and idiomatic expressions, so the message truly connects. This isn't just practical – it's deeply pastoral: it removes barriers and affirms that the Gospel is for everyone.

> *"Act as a translation expert in Spanish and Portuguese with solid theological background. Translate this devotional from Spanish to Portuguese for a Brazilian community, adapting urban Latin American cultural references to their context. Keep the tone pastoral and simple."*

Keyword and Thematic Biblical Analysis

Another powerful use is lexical and thematic analysis. A pastor or teacher can ask AI to identify repeated words in a chapter, their theological relevance, Hebrew or Greek roots, and connections to other biblical texts. This allows for richer, more contextual, comparative studies.

Until recently, only highly developed tools like Logos Bible Software could do this, connecting themes across a vast library. But now, AI chatbots make this accessible to everyone, without expensive software.

> *"Analyze the word 'hope' in Romans 5. Explain its Greek root, where else it appears in the New Testament, and its theological significance within the broader Pauline literature."*

AI can also group related passages, assist in preparing inductive studies, and suggest Old/New Testament connections that may be missed in a superficial reading.

Comparative Study of Bible Translations

For those teaching in multilingual contexts, comparing different translations is essential. AI can align verses from versions like the KJV, NIV, ESV, NRSB, and NET, highlight meaningful differences, and recommend the best fit for a specific purpose – such as memorization, theological study, or public reading.

Some multimodal models also allow voice interaction, so you do not even need to type.

> *"Compare Romans 8:1 in the KJV, NIV, and NRSB. Explain differences in tone and emphasis and recommend which would be most suitable for a group of young people new to the faith."*

In the hands of a Spirit-led community, these tools are not only efficient – they're missional. They allow more people, in more places, to better understand the Scriptures. And the better we understand, the more deeply we love. And the more we love, the more faithfully we live.

Used wisely, AI can be like the helpers of Ezra in Nehemiah 8:8, who "read from the Book of the Law of God, making it clear and giving the meaning so that the people understood what was being read." Today, with screens instead of scrolls, we can do the same.

It's important to say that we must not use AI models without a critical filter, nor should we rest our biblical interpretation and application entirely on their responses. I'll return to this in the chapter on **Cyberintelligent Wisdom and Ethics**. We still depend on the guidance of the Holy Spirit and the wisdom we ask from God, so that the Word may shape us. As the Lord said:

> But when he, the Spirit of truth, comes, he will guide you into all the truth. He will not speak on his own; he will speak only what he hears, and he will tell you what is yet to come (John 16:13).

And as James added:

> If any of you lacks wisdom, you should ask God, who gives generously to all without finding fault, and it will be given to you (James 1:5).

Learning with Humility

St. Teresa of Jesus said, "Humility is truth." This is deeply meaningful in the context of learning and becoming a disciple of the Lord. Without humility, we cannot recognize our need for help in growing in Him, nor can we imitate His character when He said:

> Take my yoke upon you and learn from me, for I am gentle and humble in heart, and you will find rest for your souls (Matthew 11:29).

Christian learning has never been about accumulating information but about shaping the soul – from the disciples who walked the roads with Jesus to copyists like Diemoth (whose Germanic name, incidentally, means "humility"). Every word was a prayer, and every lesson was an act of reverence, not of utility. In Hebrew tradition, learning wasn't a means to mastery – it was a means to worship. Wisdom was not instrumental – it was sacred.

Today, the modern world learns to use, to optimize, and to apply. But in the Kingdom of God, we still learn to worship. AI can provide us with data, structures, translations, and connections. It can help us teach clearly, prepare quickly, and explain accurately. But it can never instill wonder, nor awaken humility.

That's why the challenge is not only to teach with smarter tools, but with more surrendered hearts. AI cannot replace the Master – but it can serve as a faithful scribe to the eternal message. Just like those who prepared scrolls with devotion, we too must prepare each lesson with holy fear and eternal purpose.

To recover the heart of learning as discipleship is to see every word taught as a seed of the Kingdom, and every classroom – whether physical or digital – as holy ground. Let our teachings not only inform, but form. Not only explain but transform.

So let us teach with excellence – because God deserves it – and learn with humility – because we need it. In cyber-intelligent learning, what matters is not how much technology we use, but how much our hearts resemble the Master we follow.

Christian learning has never been about accumulating information but about shaping the soul

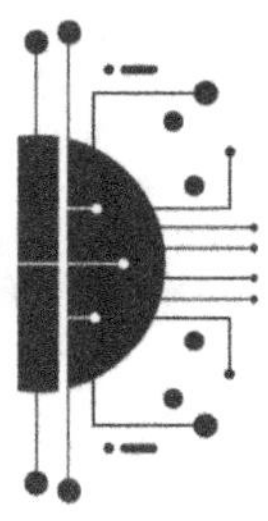

Now, here is an instruction designed for leaders, teachers, or pastors who want to use artificial intelligence to plan a Bible lesson. This prompt encourages thoughtful, spiritually grounded use.

> *"Act as a biblical teacher with pastoral sensitivity, theological knowledge, and discipleship experience.*
>
> *Help me plan a teaching for adults new to the faith on the topic: 'God's Faithfulness in Times of Trial,' based on Lamentations 3:21–26 and James 1:2–4.*
>
> *Please suggest:*
>
> *– A three-part teaching outline (introduction, development, application), with brief titles.*
> *– Reflection questions that encourage group dialogue.*
> *– A creative activity or spiritual exercise to reinforce the lesson.*
> *– A final prayer to close the session with hope and trust in God.*
>
> *Maintain a warm, biblically sound tone, and make it adaptable for a group of 8 to 12 people. Also create a downloadable PowerPoint presentation outline."*

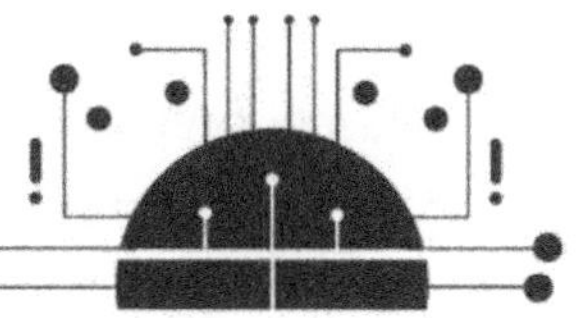

CYBERINTELLIGENT ANNOUNCING

Those who can imagine anything,
can create the impossible.[13]

– ALAN TURING, BRITISH MATHEMATICIAN.

Every place where God leads,
there is your field.

– DWIGHT L. MOODY, RADIO EVANGELIST.

A never-ending stream of encrypted words flowed from the command centers of the Third Reich to its military units. Each message was an instrument of war. Each code, a barrier. The Enigma machine,[14] with its rotors and wiring, created a cipher so complex that no one had been able to break it.

The messages came daily.

In code.

Impenetrable.

Until he appeared.

His name was Alan Turing – a British mathematician, eccentric and tireless – who arrived at Bletchley Park with a single obsession: to break the code that was sustaining chaos. He wasn't seeking fame – only understanding. His aim wasn't to destroy, but to save. To accomplish this, he designed a machine to read hidden signals. It wasn't immediately. It wasn't perfect. But it worked. Thanks to his invention, the Allies began intercepting enemy communications, anticipating their movements, and eventually shifting the tide of the war. It's estimated that his work shortened the conflict by at least two years and saved millions of lives.

Not with weapons.

With understanding.

Today, we're not at war with nations, but we are at war with the darkness that keeps many far from the truth. People still send encrypted signals, even if it's not obvious. A cynical comment on social media may be a hidden cry for hope. A cold question like "what's the point of religion?" may conceal a history of betrayal, abandonment, or pain. No one walks into the world saying, "I'm ready to believe." They arrive with their own version of Enigma – unspoken wounds, cultural barriers, emotional codes, hardened prejudices, or hidden sin.

And there stands the Church – reading the stream of words, gestures, algorithms, statistics. Watching. Praying. Trying to decode.

How do we reach those who do not speak our spiritual language?

How do we translate the Gospel for hearts drowning in noise?

Maybe it's time to build our own redeemed version of Bletchley Park.

AI isn't Turing. It doesn't have his humanity or compassion. But it can be a tool like the one he created – a way of reading between the lines, of listening beyond the words, of anticipating need. AI tools can help us detect patterns in the questions people ask online. They can help us respond with gentleness and truth to those who are unknowingly searching. They can help us adapt the eternal message to the rhythm and language of this generation. Not to manipulate – but to understand. Not to control – but to save.

Just as Turing decoded messages to save lives, today the Church can use AI to interpret the modern cries of the heart for meaning, community, and redemption. It's not about predicting conversions – but preparing answers. Not about replacing witnesses – but amplifying their voices.

Every automated conversation can be a doorway.

Every chatbot, a seed.

Every generated image, a reflection of an unspoken question.

And while AI can't preach the Gospel in spirit and truth, it can help create the space for that preaching to happen. It can build bridges for those who no longer enter churches but still scroll through timelines. To those who do not read the Bible but seek answers through search engines. To those who have shut the door on religious language but left a window open in the form of likes, comments, or search queries.

Alan Turing never knew how many lives he saved. He simply fulfilled his task: to read what was hidden, understand what seemed incomprehensible, and return a bit of hope to the world.

We, however, do know what message has been entrusted to our hands: the good news is that there is a Savior. And perhaps today, part of our mission is to use every available tool to ensure that message finds its way through the maze of the modern soul – decoded, clear, and true – into the heart that needs it.

Not all codes are military.

Some are spiritual.

And the Gospel remains the only message capable of breaking any silence.

An Eternal Message for an Encrypted World

Alan Turing was not only the genius who helped decipher Nazi Germany's codes; he was also the father of modern computing and one of the conceptual pioneers of artificial intelligence. Long before personal computers or virtual assistants, Turing proposed the idea of a "universal machine" capable of executing any logical calculation – what we now know as the Turing machine.

But his brilliance went beyond mathematics. Turing asked a deeply philosophical question: Can a machine think? To explore this, he proposed a thought experiment known as the Turing Test, in which a computer would be considered intelligent if it could convince a human that it was human. His famous assertion summarized it:

> "A computer should be considered intelligent if it can deceive a human into believing it is human."

Today, that idea feels eerily familiar. Virtual assistants converse with ease. AI can generate empathetic responses. Some people even admit to forming emotional bonds with automated systems. But while Turing framed this as an intellectual challenge, the Church faces a deeper spiritual one – not whether machines can appear human, but whether humans can continue to reflect the image of God in an increasingly artificial world.

In this context, evangelism has become a more complex discipline. We're no longer up against overt persecution or doctrinal censorship. We face cultural, social, and existential codes that obscure the Gospel. People aren't opposed to the message – they simply do not understand it. Or they do not find it relevant. They do not speak "our spiritual language." They use different categories. They're encrypted.

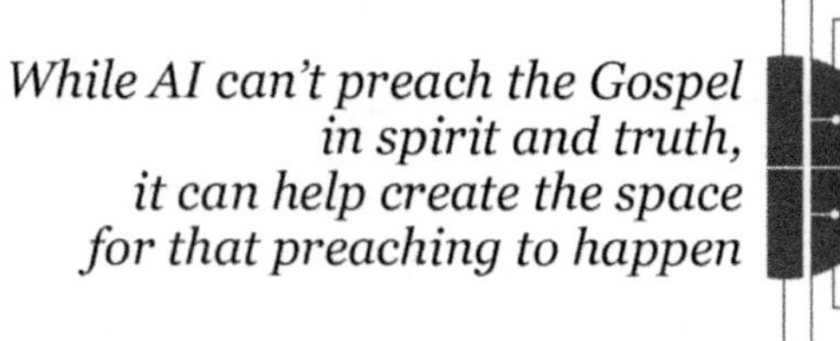

A college student may not ask "How can I be saved?" – but they will type into Google: "Why do I feel empty when I have everything?"

An agnostic adult may never set foot in a church – but they spend hours on social media searching for content on purpose, anxiety, forgiveness, or hope.

The questions are there – encrypted in the emotional and digital language of this generation – but they need to be deciphered so that the eternal message can be heard.

The Church, then, is called to a task that echoes Turing's challenge: to read between the lines, to listen beyond the words, and to find the right channels to translate the Gospel – without distorting it. Instead of chasing the illusion of a machine that seems human, we should pursue a Church that is more human, more compassionate, and more capable of listening with spiritual discernment.

In this endeavor, AI can serve not as a substitute for the missionary, but as an assistant to the evangelist. It can help us identify search patterns, analyze social media comments, and interpret the emotions behind the questions. It can help us get organized, focus on relevant topics, and communicate in cultural languages that connect with diverse audiences.

But there is a crucial difference:

AI can simulate empathy, but it cannot feel compassion.

It can recognize patterns of pain, but it cannot carry them.

It can generate responses, but it cannot offer comfort.

That task remains fully human – and deeply spiritual.

That's why the challenge of this generation isn't merely to "use AI to evangelize," but to discern how to translate the eternal message in a coded world – saturated with information but starving for truth. The Church doesn't need to compete with algorithms. It needs to learn how to read the modern soul with redeemed eyes – and find faithful ways to communicate the good news to those who do not even know they're waiting for it.

The Gospel remains the power of God for salvation (Romans 1:16) – but it must be preached in the language of the heart, not just the language of the temple. And if artificial intelligence can help us identify the soul's keywords, then it becomes a tool worthy of redemption for the sake of the mission.

New Public Squares

In Athens, Paul did not wait for people to come to the temple. Instead, he went out to meet them in the spaces where they thought, lived, and searched for meaning. Upon arriving in the city, the text says that "he was greatly distressed to see that the city was full of idols" (Acts 17:16). But rather than condemning it from afar, Paul began to dialogue "in the synagogue with both Jews and God-fearing Greeks, as well as in the marketplace day by day with those who happened to be there" (v.17). It was in the public square – the agora – where he engaged with Epicurean and Stoic philosophers, who eventually brought him to the Areopagus, the city's intellectual center.

There, Paul did not preach using Jewish religious formulas nor did he repeat his testimony out of context. He began with a cultural observation:

> People of Athens! I see that in every way you are very religious. For as I walked around and looked carefully

> at your objects of worship, I even found an altar with this inscription: TO AN UNKNOWN GOD. So you are ignorant of the very thing you worship – and this is what I am going to proclaim to you (Acts 17:22–23).

Paul didn't dilute the truth, but he did contextualize it, translating it into the language, philosophy, and sensitivity of his audience.

This episode remains a valid missionary model for the digital age. Social media are our new Areopagi: spaces where multiple beliefs, voices, aspirations, and confusions coexist. We cannot expect people to "come to the digital temple." Like Paul, we must go to the square, observe with spiritual discernment, and engage in dialogue with wisdom and compassion. The unknown God is still being sought – though now He is sought in hashtags, forums, comments, and shared posts.

Today, those squares are made not of stone but of pixels. Their names are Instagram, TikTok, YouTube, Facebook, WhatsApp, Reddit, X. They are the spaces where people – especially the young – gather, not so much physically, but emotionally and culturally. There, they share their struggles, doubts, joys, and their emptiness.

For the Church, these platforms represent a new mission frontier, a digital Areopagus we cannot ignore. But unlike the ancient squares, these host millions of simultaneous conversations – and that's where artificial intelligence can offer a strategic lens.

AI as an Extended Pastoral Ear

One of the most useful capacities of artificial intelligence is its ability to analyze large volumes of data in real time. AI-based tools can identify emerging spiritual trends, detect keywords that express pain or seeking, and suggest optimal times to post relevant content.

For example, by monitoring public conversations around topics like anxiety, purpose, or hopelessness, it's possible to generate pastoral content that responds not with religious propaganda but with compassionate presence.

> *"Analyze recent social media posts among young people ages 18 to 25 expressing feelings of anxiety or loss of purpose. Suggest five ideas for Christian content that offers hope, using authentic and culturally relevant language."*

Sowing Without Losing the Soul

AI can also assist in creating visual messages, graphics, short videos, and applied biblical texts designed to connect with specific audiences. This doesn't mean fabricating emotion but translating the message with sensitivity: the Gospel remains; the language changes.

Example applications:

- Devotionals in reel format
- Micro-testimonies as visual narratives
- Animated explainers in generational language
- Open-ended questions that invite spiritual dialogue, not dogmatic debate.

But there's a risk here too: the temptation to reduce the message to the algorithm. Platforms reward what is emotional, viral, immediate. The Church must resist the pressure to dilute truth for visibility. AI can help – but the voice of the Spirit doesn't follow the logic of likes.

Automation with Discernment

Some churches already use AI to auto-respond to messages on their pages or accounts. These bots can greet, offer resources, direct to devotionals, or ask guiding questions. They're useful, especially when paired with human pastoral follow-up.

However, every automated process must be reviewed with pastoral discernment. The goal is not to simulate a spiritual conversation but to open a real door for one. While AI can "talk," only the Holy Spirit can convict, comfort, and regenerate.

Social media is not the enemy of faith. Nor is it neutral. It's an open stage where thousands of souls express their pain and dreams every hour. The question is not whether we should be there, but how we can be present with integrity, beauty, and truth. With the help of AI, we can sharpen our hearing, extend our voice, and plant the eternal message with cultural precision – without losing its spiritual essence.

The square is still full. The Gospel is still relevant. We just need to listen wisely and speak compassionately.

I invite you to explore how AI can help you create regular social media content. Test this approach with an initial instruction that defines a framework:

> *"Act as a social media strategist and community manager to create a content framework that includes inspirational, instructional, informative, and missional content to be posted over one week."*

Adapt it with your own values. Then ask it to generate an instruction for automating content creation like this:

"Act as a Christian communicator with pastoral experience, solid biblical knowledge, and cultural sensitivity for social media.

Help me plan a week of social media posts using this thematic framework:
Monday – Inspirational
Tuesday – Instructional
Wednesday – Missional (evangelistic)
Thursday – Relational (community engagement)
Friday – Instructional (devotional or spiritual resource)
Saturday –Informative / Pastoral (announcements or practical guides)
Sunday – Liturgical / Inspirational (connected to Sunday's message or worship)

The biblical theme for the week will be: 'God's Faithfulness Amid Change', based on Lamentations 3:22–23, Hebrews 13:8, and Isaiah 41:10.

For each day, please generate:

A short main post text (max 50 words)

A Bible verse or reference

A suggested hashtag or call to action

An ideal format (image, short video, story, etc.) Use a warm, contemporary, pastoral tone. The content should be accessible to both believers and seekers. Avoid complex religious jargon. Emojis can be used sparingly if appropriate".

Evangelists at the Digital Door

Just a few years ago, it was hard to imagine someone asking a spiritual question at 2 a.m. – and getting an answer immediately. Today that's possible, not because of the pastor's omnipresence, but through AI-powered virtual assistants that can attend, guide, and walk with a seeker in the moment of their search.

Far from replacing the pastoral ministry, these chatbots can become digital gatekeepers of faith: they do not replace the community, but they can open the first door.

Real-Time Conversational Evangelism

At the heart of this approach is the idea of constant, contextual availability. Many people wouldn't step into a church – but would start an anonymous digital conversation. There they ask real questions, from places of confusion or pain:

- "Does God really exist?"
- "Why do I feel empty?"
- "Can I be forgiven after what I've done?"
- "Does God hear me if I do not go to church?"

These aren't theology exams. They're cries from the soul. Try to use these as a guided exercise in prompt refinement to explore the AI chatbot answers in different theological context.

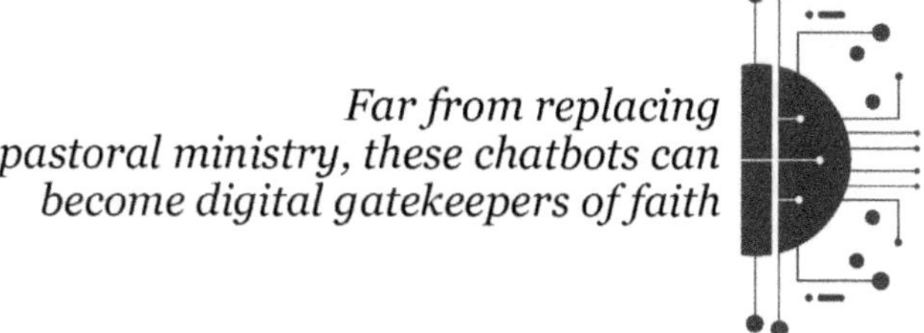

> *"Act as a Christian mentor with compassion, biblical knowledge, and clarity. Create short and accessible responses to these three frequently asked questions from faith seekers:*
>
> *Why does God allow suffering?*
> *What does it mean to follow Jesus?*
> *How do I know that God forgives me?*
>
> *Use simple language, include a biblical reference, and end each response with an invitation to dialogue or community"*

When a church has a virtual assistant well-trained in biblical, sensitive, and pastoral content, it can respond with truth and compassion even when no human is available. In many cases, these conversations lead to follow-up relationships with real leaders.

Ethical Design and Training

A chatbot should not pretend to be human. Its role is not to simulate faith but to facilitate access to the message of faith. Its design must be clear, honest, and respectful. It is advisable to inform the user that they are interacting with artificial intelligence. Still, with proper training, it can act as a digital guide that accompanies the first steps toward discipleship.

This type of tool can be integrated into:

- Ministry websites
- Messaging platforms like WhatsApp, Messenger, or Telegram
- Discipleship applications
- Automated evangelistic campaigns.

Responses should be based on clear doctrinal principles and reviewed by ministry leaders. Additionally, it should include escalation protocols: if a person expresses a need for counseling, emotional crisis, or a desire to follow Christ, the system should alert a human. AI can start the conversation – but the pastoral body must complete it.

Open Doors in the Culture of Immediacy

We live in a time where immediate responses are expected for every concern. As ministries struggle with full schedules and limited resources, virtual assistants can be a bridge – a first "yes" to someone who didn't know how to approach.

These "digital evangelists" will never replace the warmth of human conversation – nor should they. But they can plant seeds, guide, and listen. They can be the voice that says, "we're here for you" when no one else responds. And in that availability, they reflect something of the character of the One who neither sleeps nor leaves.

The Great Commission isn't confined to work hours or office schedules. If we are called to reach "to the ends of the earth" (Acts 1:8), we must also be willing to reach the last notification. Virtual assistants and chatbots, when well-designed and ethically guided, can become silent servants – like Philip beside the Ethiopian's chariot – running alongside the modern cart: the phone, the screen, the search – and gently asking, "Do you understand what you are reading?" (Acts 8:30).

Missional Strategy

Evangelizing is not just about speaking – it's about discerning when, how, to whom, and with what words. Jesus himself modeled this situational wisdom: He didn't teach the same way in the synagogue as He did in an open field, nor did He respond the same to the rich young man as He did to the Samaritan woman. His message was constant, but His approach adapted precisely to the listener's heart.

Today, churches have access to data that allows for the same kind of contextual discernment – at scale. Artificial intelligence can act as a strategic assistant for mission, analyzing environments, audiences, digital consumption habits, and cultural touchpoints.

Missional Segmentation: Beyond Demographics

AI platforms can process large volumes of public data: search habits, spiritual content consumption patterns, recurring interests by region, age, or language. This enables churches to detect underserved populations or those especially open to the Gospel.

One leading platform in this field is Gloo, a digital ecosystem that helps churches connect with spiritual seekers through smart segmentation and contextual data.

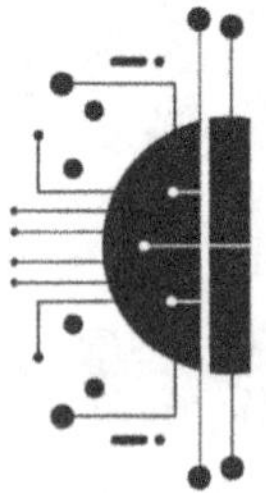

Evangelizing is not just about speaking —it's about discerning when, how, to whom, and with what words

Instead of limiting by age or location, Gloo provides deeper insights: spiritual interests, life moments (such as grief, anxiety, relationship restoration), and digital search patterns. This enables the design of personalized evangelistic messages, the assignment of relevant resources, and – most importantly – building bridges between people's real needs and the Gospel's response. More than a marketing tool, Gloo expands what's possible for digital-era missional outreach.

And this is only the beginning. I'm convinced that the power of AI will grow as more platforms specialize in the broader historical and theological context of churches using AI.

For example, an urban church may discover that its community has a large population of young adults consuming mental health and spirituality content – but not following religious accounts. That's a missional door waiting to be opened.

> *"Suggest a three-phase digital strategy to launch an evangelistic campaign aimed at young adults (ages 20–30) in large cities who show interest in emotional health but have no connection to churches. The tone should be empathetic, non-religious, and include opportunities for personal follow-up."*

Cultural and Linguistic Localization

Recently, I had the chance to attend the *Latino Media Summit*, part of NRB's annual conference.[15] There, I saw significant advancements in enabling live event translations into multiple languages using AI-powered applications and devices. Soon – already unfolding before our eyes – our wireless earbuds may be the only interpreters we need.

AI also enables evangelistic messages to be contextualized into multiple languages, dialects, and cultures. It's not just about translating words – but adjusting references, metaphors, and questions to suit the audience's sensitivity.

This is especially valuable in missionary ministries, transnational churches, and global digital communities. The Gospel is eternal, but it has never been monolingual.

For instance, the same evangelistic video can be automatically adapted into five languages and cultural tones, respecting visual cues, examples, and social norms using existing video-to-voice, voice-to-voice, or text-to-speech tools. You could even prompt AI to suggest cultural adaptations and localizations that will make your videos more appropriate in the context.

Personalized Spiritual Pathways

AI tools make it possible to offer discipleship paths tailored to each user's interest and spiritual level. Based on their interactions, AI can propose:

- Devotional video series
- Introductory courses on the Christian faith
- Bible reading challenges
- Connection to a human mentor.

This doesn't replace traditional discipleship – but it can initiate or strengthen it, especially where in-person Christian community is unavailable.

> *"Design a basic digital discipleship path for a new believer who has just expressed faith in Christ. Include 5 steps with short resources (videos, texts, prayers) and an option to connect with a mentor."*

AI as Pastoral Radar

Finally, AI can function as a kind of spiritual radar for the church. It can detect changes in emotional language within comments, track when an audience becomes more receptive, or highlight emerging topics that need a biblical response.

For example, after a national crisis or natural disaster, it can help the church respond quickly with comfort, prayer, and direct content.

The same Spirit who guided Philip toward the Ethiopian (Acts 8:26–29) can guide the church today through new signals – and AI can be one of those instruments. Not as an oracle, but as a tool in service of the vision. Like sundials, compasses, or maps used by past missionaries, this technology is not the calling itself – but it can help us respond with precision and purpose.

A church that listens well, communicates better. And in a world overflowing with words but starving for meaning, a mission strategy powered by AI isn't a luxury – it's faithful stewardship.

The Universal Key

In every era, God has provided His people with tools to fulfill their mission. From Paul's handwritten letters to Gutenberg's press, from evangelistic radio to digital channels, the Gospel message has always found ways to cross cultural, geographic, and generational barriers.

Today, we live in a time where information is abundant, but meaning is scarce. The voices may be many, but the truth may drown in the noise. That's where the church is called to reclaim its evangelistic heart – not as an optional task, but as the living expression of its identity. The Great Commission still stands.

Technology does not replace it – but it can help make it more visible, more accessible, and bolder.

Just as Turing broke a code to save lives, the church can use artificial intelligence to break through digital noise, cultural confusion, and emotional skepticism – to clearly proclaim the unchanging good news: Jesus Christ saves. The Gospel remains the universal key to the human soul. And every new tool we have – if used with discernment and humility – can become a new doorway for its arrival.

Today, we live in a time where information is abundant, but meaning is scarce

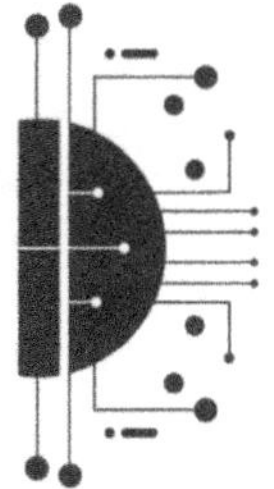

AI is not an end. It's a means. In redeemed hands, it can become an intelligent extension of divine compassion – reaching those who do not yet know they're being sought by the God who became Word to find them.

If God is calling you to use AI to reach others, as Moody said, "there is your field."

If you've read this far, you've likely sensed that artificial intelligence opens a world of possibilities. One of the most common comments I hear from students in the Inteliagentes program (https://inteliagentes.com) is that interacting with AI sparks their creativity. With the concepts I've shared and the prompt suggestions I've offered, I hope I've created the same effect on you.

Before continuing to the next chapter on cyberintelligent assistance, I want to leave you with a prompt you can use as a model to create a weekly plan for evangelistic social media posts.

Act as a missionary strategist with pastoral sensitivity, biblical knowledge, and digital experience.

Help me design a week of evangelistic social media posts aimed at people who do not attend church but show interest in topics like anxiety, life purpose, and spirituality.

For each day, suggest:

A content idea (short video, image, story, question, quote)

A brief text centered on the message of the Gospel, without religious jargon

An empathetic call to action (comment, share, write, respond)

An ideal format (reel, image, carousel, audio)

Use compassionate, hopeful, and culturally relevant language. The goal is to open meaningful conversations – not to impose answers."

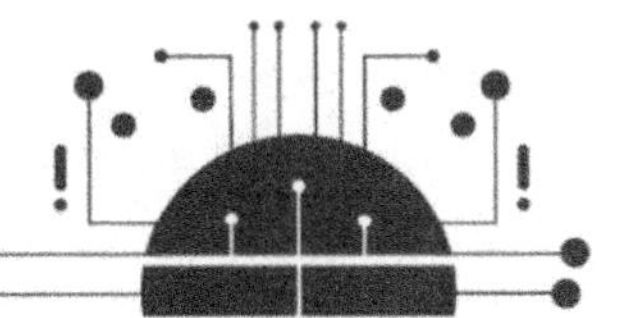

CYBERINTELLIGENT ASSISTING

Not all the arts... have yet been found: "There are many which have not yet been discovered. Every day you could find one, and there will still be new ones to find."[16]

– FR. GIORDANO OF PISA, DOMINICAN MONK.

Optics, developing in us through study, teach us to see.

– PAUL CEZANNE, FRENCH PAINTER.

The air smelled of old incense and damp stone. In the central nave of Santa Maria Novella, the afternoon light filtered through the stained glass, casting purple and gold across the garments of the faithful. The Dominican friar's voice rang out from the pulpit – firm, clear, and wrapped in the kind of echo only a Gothic temple can produce. The year was 1306, and Florence was a vibrant city, pulsing with commerce, intrigue, and learning.

Friar Giordano of Pisa was known not only for his eloquence but also for his ability to see in human inventions a sign of God's providential movement. That day, however, he wasn't preaching about heresies or doctrines, but about a new object that was causing astonishment among senior clergy: eyeglasses.

"Less than twenty years ago," he preached, "the art of making eyeglasses was discovered to help us see better, an art that is one of the best and most necessary in the world. And it wasn't long ago that this new art, which had never existed, was invented... I saw the man who discovered it and practiced it, and I was able to speak with him."[17]

Friar Giordano's words were not laced with suspicion, but with gratitude. He did not fear innovation. On the contrary, he celebrated it as a manifestation of common grace – a gift from God that didn't replace the soul's vision but eased the burden of those who could no longer read, teach, or copy the Scriptures.

Then, as if led deeper by the Spirit, he compared the invention to the soul itself:

> There are three kinds of mirrors: one is convex, which we use, and which makes things appear smaller than they are. Another is flat, which reflects things as they are. The third is concave, which shows the image upside down, like topaz, I believe he said. And the reason is this: the saints say its nature, its growth, goes in reverse. And you must know that any mirror must be pure, otherwise it will reflect nothing.[18]

He was not only talking about glass. He was talking about the human heart. About how we perceive reality. How we see others, God, and ourselves. How even the help we offer is shaped by the clarity of our vision.

More than seven centuries have passed since that homily, yet the problem remains the same: the need to see clearly to care well.

Today, it's not eye fatigue that most limits pastors, but emotional fatigue, ministry overload, and the difficulty of deeply attending to each person crying out from their digital corner or hidden need. Letters no longer arrive by courier, but by notification. Confessions do not always happen in temples – they arrive in chats, emails, comments, and anonymous forms.

And again, a new tool has emerged. Not as tangible as glasses but designed to assist vision: artificial intelligence. A technology that, when well-trained and consecrated to purpose, can help ministries of compassion to see more clearly – to detect patterns of suffering, offer initial guidance, better organize care, and be present when the human cannot.

Like the first spectacles, it does not replace the soul nor the touch. But it can return to the church the ability to focus care on those who need it most.

This chapter explores how AI can assist in pastoral care, crisis support, ministry to the marginalized, and the ethical challenges that arise when technology enters the spaces of the soul. Because just as mirrors must be pure to reflect faithfully, our tools must also be pure in intent, firm in truth, and full of grace.

For to help others see more clearly... has always been, in the Church, an act of love.

Vision and Pastoral Presence

The first glasses did not heal the eyes but restored clarity. They were a technological act of mercy – a way to restore the ability to read, to teach, to see others. In a way, they were an embodied pastoral act: a simple aid born in the heart of the Church, yet deeply meaningful for those who had begun to lose the ability to focus.

So too is the pastoral vocation: a ministry of vision – not to control, but to care. At its core, compassion begins with open eyes.

When Jesus walked through villages, He didn't just preach.

> When he saw the crowds, he had compassion on them, because they were harassed and helpless, like sheep without a shepherd (Matthew 9:36).

His care flowed from His gaze, as a deeply human and divine reaction to visible suffering. In another passage, Mark records:

> When Jesus landed and saw a large crowd, he had compassion on them, because they were like sheep without a shepherd. So he began teaching them many things (Mark 6:34).

In both cases, compassion didn't begin with touch – or even with words. It began with seeing. And not merely noticing but recognizing. Recognizing need, abandonment, emptiness – and then acting with tenderness.

A pastor, in the most biblical sense, is not just one who speaks from a pulpit, but one who sees and does not pass by – one who stays. He is like the Samaritan in Jesus' parable.

> But a Samaritan, as he traveled, came where the man was; and when he saw him, he took pity on him (Luke 10:33).

This act of seeing is not automatic. It is learned, cultivated, and refined. That's why Friar Giordano spoke not only of lenses but also of mirrors, just as the apostle Paul did:

> For now, we see only a reflection as in a mirror; then we shall see face to face. Now I know in part; then I shall know fully. (1 Corinthians 13:12).

Pastoral vision, too, must be refined and purified. A heart distorted by pride will see people as problems. A heart wounded by bitterness will see them as threats. But a heart aligned with Christ will see them as souls in need of grace.

John the Baptist understood his role this way:

> He himself was not the light; he came only as a witness to the light (John 1:8).

And we, in pastoral work, are not the source of light, but mirrors that reflect it. Our task is to look with redeemed eyes, to listen with undivided attention, and to act not for efficiency, but for love.

Today, needs show up in new forms. They do not always enter through the church doors; they often arrive via inbox, website chat, or anonymous prayer request forms. And if our vision is not sharpened, we may not see. We may overlook signs of distress, despair, or vulnerability.

That's why when we talk about AI in pastoral care, we're not talking about replacement – but about tools that help us see better: modern-day lenses for the digital era.

In fact, AI, as part of the technological continuum, has become necessary. In an era where information flows at an unprecedented speed and scale, AI is no longer a luxury but a strategic pastoral response.

Diemoth – whom I mentioned in **Chapter 3** – devoted her entire life to producing just 45 illuminated manuscripts. Today, one person with a smartphone generates more than 1.5 gigabytes of data per day through texts, images, locations, searches, and conversations. Globally, it's estimated that humanity produces over 328 million terabytes of data every day. Only artificial intelligence can process that overwhelming stream of data and make sense of it.

Now imagine what it takes to discern signals of distress, loneliness, or spiritual need. Surely it requires more than goodwill and surface-level data interpretation – it requires compassionate technological assistance. AI does not replace pastoral discernment, but it can help us focus better, see more clearly, and not lose sight of those crying out amid the noise.

Like 21st-century spectacles, these technologies – when well guided – can help us detect, organize, and respond with greater precision. They do not make us more spiritual, but they can make us more available, more attentive, and more effective in shepherding the flock entrusted to us. Jesus said:

> "I am the good shepherd; I know my sheep and my sheep know me." (John 10:14, NIV)

And knowing begins with seeing – clearly, purely, compassionately.

Pastoral Ally

The image of the shepherd with staff and rod is tender, but incomplete when applied to the complexity of the modern world. Today, the flock is scattered across physical and digital spaces, and the signs of suffering no longer always appear as visible tears but as fragmented patterns: prolonged silences, virtual absences, changes in language, or anonymous searches.

In this context, pastoral care needs more eyes and ears – but also more hands to process, organize, and prioritize.

This is where artificial intelligence can serve as a faithful assistant – not as a replacement for human touch, but as a practical extension of pastoral care, especially in large or digitally distributed communities. When implemented well, AI can help in three key areas: organization, early detection, and compassionate follow-up.

Organizing Requests and Follow-Up

One of the most immediate functions of AI in ministry settings is the classification of requests: prayer forms, direct messages, counseling inquiries, meeting notes. What once could get stuck in inboxes or rely on an exhausted leader's memory can now be automatically organized by topic, urgency, or designated ministry team.

AI can generate prioritized lists, suggest initial responses, and even schedule follow-up reminders so that no need is left unaddressed.

Practical example: A pastoral team may receive over 100 prayers or help requests in a week. AI can group them into categories (illness, relationships, finances, faith) and identify patterns – such as an unusual increase in messages related to anxiety. This enables leadership not only to respond individually but to plan a series of teachings or community gatherings around that theme.

> *"Act as a digital pastoral assistant. Organize this list of 100 requests according to common themes (e.g., health, grief, faith, relationships). Indicate the perceived level of urgency and suggest a basic response or referral plan. Provide the results in a table."*

Early Detection of Spiritual or Emotional Patterns

Beyond logistics, AI can assist in detecting collective emotional or spiritual trends. By analyzing the language used in messages or posts within digital communities, it can identify terms linked to suffering, isolation, spiritual fatigue, or even suicidal ideation. This doesn't replace pastoral discernment but offers early signals that can trigger timely human responses.

Additionally, AI can help accompany new believers, detecting recurring questions or common insecurities and suggesting discipleship materials or connecting them with spiritual mentors.

For example: In a church with an active digital ministry, AI identifies that many people are asking about forgiveness. The system sends an alert and proposes recent content on the topic or notifies the pastoral team to address the need in upcoming teachings.

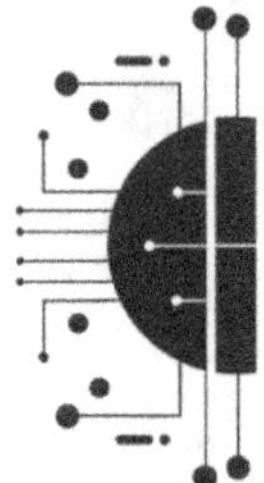

AI can help accompany new believers, detecting recurring questions or common insecurities and suggesting discipleship materials

Constant Care in High-Demand Contexts

In times of crisis, AI can help manage overwhelming pastoral demands. During emergencies – such as collective loss, natural disasters, or moments of social upheaval – requests may exceed the capacity of the human team. An AI assistant can:

- Confirm immediate receipt of requests.
- Share immediate support resources (prayers, Scripture, encouragement videos).
- Automatically classify urgent cases and escalate them to human leaders when necessary.

This not only improves efficiency but also communicates a sense of constant presence and care, which is essential in digital pastoral ministry.

The Good Shepherd knows His sheep, but He also knows how to search for them when they are lost. In a world where the flock moves at digital speed, the pastoral heart needs intelligent support to leave no one behind. AI doesn't see as we do – but it can help us see what often goes unnoticed. And in Spirit-led hands, that kind of vision can mean the difference between a forgotten request and a soul cared for.

Crisis Management

There are moments when human need doesn't wait for office hours, nor can it be funneled through forms. Anxiety surfaces in the early morning hours, grief arrives in the silence of a Sunday afternoon, and despair knocks on the soul's door in the solitude of a room connected to the world but disconnected from any community. Pastoral care, in these moments, requires presence, availability, and a word – even when the pastor is asleep or far away.

This is where AI, used with sensitivity and wisdom, can provide an initial form of accompaniment – extending the arms of comfort digitally, not pretending to replace incarnate presence, but sustaining it until it's possible.

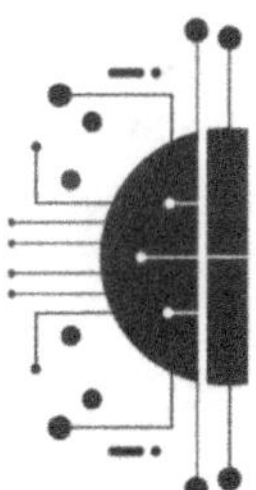

AI, used with sensitivity and wisdom, can provide an initial form of accompaniment

Chatbots Trained for Spiritual Care

Chatbots can be trained to recognize and respond to common existential questions with biblical, empathetic, and non-invasive replies. Functioning 24/7, they can handle initial conversations with those seeking guidance, relief, or simply someone to listen. They are not counselors, but initial bridges to true comfort.

These systems can ask open-ended questions, suggest appropriate Bible passages, share brief prayers, or recommend resources based on expressed needs. At all times, they must clearly indicate they are automated and offer options to connect with human counselors.

> *"Create a conversation flow for someone who writes: 'I do not want to keep living like this.' The chatbot should respond with sensitivity, offer immediate emotional support, suggest helpful resources, and encourage seeking pastoral or professional help. Avoid heavy theological content; focus on hope and accompaniment."*

Crisis Language Detection

Some AI tools, when responsibly implemented, can analyze written language in emails, prayer forms, chats, or private networks to detect signs of severe emotional suffering: suicidal thoughts, extreme anxiety, abuse, or abandonment.

These tools do not diagnose but can alert trained leaders for timely intervention. They are especially useful in large churches, online communities, or discipleship platforms where the volume of interaction may cause subtle cries for help to go unnoticed.

For example: A church with an active youth group online configures a chatbot that detects phrases like "I'm worthless" or "It'd be better if I weren't here." When such expressions appear, the system flags the message and refers it to the assigned youth pastor, who receives a confidential alert and can act promptly.

Personalized Resource Recommendations

Another pastorally valuable function is automated generation or recommendation of resources based on expressed needs. If someone expresses feelings of loneliness, the system might send a short devotional, a guided prayer, or an invitation to a community event. If someone is grieving, it could suggest a Bible reading plan on comfort or a testimony video from someone who experienced similar loss.

In all cases, the goal is not to close the conversation, but to open a channel of grace.

> *"Act as a spiritual companion. Suggest three simple resources (a devotional, a Bible passage, and a prayer) for someone who has recently lost a loved one and feels spiritually disconnected."*

Naturally, these digital supports do not replace deep biblical counseling or long-term pastoral/therapeutic accompaniment. But they can serve as first aid – emotionally and spiritually – in moments of greatest vulnerability. They can prevent harm, initiate healing, and remind a troubled soul that it is not alone or forgotten.

Jesus not only taught us; He also wept (John 11:35). Every tool that helps us mourn with those who mourn (Romans 12:15), even if expressed through code and circuits, any tool that helps us weep with those who weep can be part of the ministry of comfort – when guided by discernment and moved by love.

Compassion and Justice with AI

Compassion in the Bible is never passive. It moves us into action. From the Old Testament through Jesus' ministry, we repeatedly encounter God's call to care for the poor, the foreigner, the widow, and the orphan. Justice, biblically speaking, is not just a legal system – it is an expression of God's character (see Micah 6:8; Isaiah 1:17; Luke 4:18).

In this context, Christian ministries working toward community help, human dignity, and social equity are a vital part of the church's mission. And while the heart of this work must always be human, AI can become a powerful ally – organizing resources better, identifying hidden needs, and acting with greater precision and efficiency.

Needs Mapping and Territorial Justice

AI can analyze demographic, social, and economic data to identify zones with high vulnerability: food insecurity, extreme poverty, social isolation, domestic violence, or lack of basic services. This enables churches and organizations to design targeted and sustainable compassionate actions.

A church can use AI to cross-reference public data with its own ministry records. They may discover, for instance, that in a neighborhood with a large senior population, no pastoral visits or volunteers are regularly present – prompting a campaign for weekly care visits.

> *"Help me identify, based on public data and social indicators, the five neighborhoods in my city with the highest levels of loneliness among older adults. Suggest a strategy for community pastoral presence adapted to those areas."*

Humanitarian Aid Optimization

When resources – food, clothes, medicine, time – are limited, they must be managed wisely. AI tools can handle inventories, coordinate deliveries, avoid duplication of efforts, and anticipate demand spikes due to emergencies (like cold waves, floods, or economic crises). This allows compassion to be more effective and responsible.

For example, a food pantry ministry might use a predictive model to analyze attendance patterns at community kitchens and based on weather or economic events, forecast an increase in demand.

Identifying the Invisible

One of the most painful challenges in compassionate ministry is that those most in need are often the quietest. People who do not ask for help, families living in the shadows of marginalization, youth without community connection. AI, using anonymized data and with respect for privacy, can detect patterns suggesting unspoken needs.

A practical example: A ministry platform discovers through digital conversation analysis that there's a migrant community not served by any church in their language. The insight becomes action: an online small group is launched, a language class is offered, or contextualized resources are distributed.

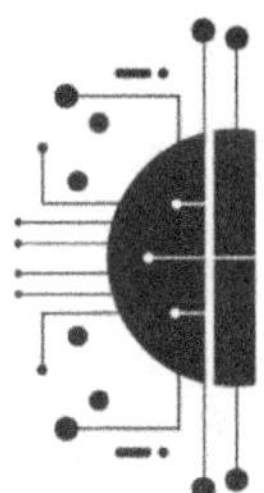

Compassion in the Bible is never passive. It moves us into action.

Sensitive Campaigns and Dignified Narratives

Finally, AI can support awareness campaigns that give voice to the voiceless. Visual content creation, empathetic writing, automated translation, and cultural adaptation are all tools that enable justice and mercy to be communicated with beauty and respect.

Pastoral Warning: Any campaign using AI must be guided by the biblical principle that every person is made in the image of God. Nothing produced should dehumanize, objectify, or exploit suffering for impact.

The parable of the Good Samaritan is not about sentiment – it's about concrete action. The Samaritan didn't have an algorithm, but he had compassionate eyes and willing hands. Today, the church can use the tools at its disposal – including AI – to better see where the wounded are, arrive faster, and care with greater consistency.

Not to glorify efficiency, but to multiply mercy.

Because if God moves among the forgotten, then technology must also bow toward them.

Seeing Better to Help Better

Like every pastoral mirror, artificial intelligence must be "pure" – transparent, clean in intent, without distortion. That was Friar Giordano's warning when speaking of the soul and knowledge: a mirror that is not clear shows nothing. In ministry, the same holds true. Any tool, no matter how advanced, loses its pastoral power if not guided by love.

Artificial intelligence can help us see more and see better: detect patterns of suffering, organize the needs of God's people, and respond with promptness and presence when human resources are limited. It can even silently uphold those who have no one else. But the action still belongs to us.

As in the parable of the Good Samaritan, Jesus does not commend the one with more knowledge, but the one who came near, saw, and acted.

> But a Samaritan, as he traveled, came where the man was; and when he saw him, he took pity on him (Luke 10:33).

That is the image of redeemed pastoral ministry: someone who sees with compassion, and whose compassion is translated into closeness – into bandages, oil, shelter, and follow-up care.

There's also an eschatological message in that story: while others passed by, one man stopped. And the one who stopped models Christ

– who does not outsource compassion but embodies it; who entrusted us with the care of the broken; and who promised to return one day to settle what remains outstanding.

The Church is called to a pastoral ministry that does not outsource care to machines, but – just as the Samaritan used wine, oil, bandages, and his donkey, the technology of his time – it uses today's tools to multiply its presence and care.

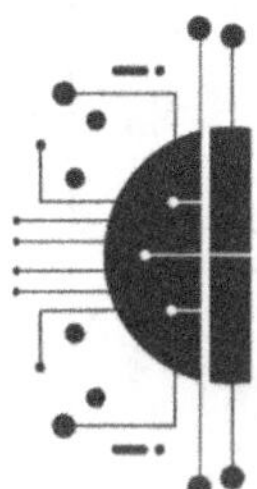

The Church is called to a pastoral ministry that does not outsource care to machines

An intelligent pastoral ministry is not merely efficient. It is deeply human. Present. Attentive. Redeemed. One that uses digital tools without abandoning the incarnational. That is guided by data yet still weeps with those who weep. That sees the neighbor not as a case, but as an image of God.

Just as glasses didn't replace the eye but helped it refocus, AI doesn't replace the pastor – but it can help them see better, to help better.

"Act as a compassionate, biblically informed, and ethically responsible pastoral assistant.

Help me plan a digital pastoral care system that includes:

- *Intake and categorization of spiritual or emotional needs.*
- *Detection of crisis patterns or warning signs.*
- *Suggested resources for support (devotionals, Scripture, prayers).*
- *Criteria for referral to human counseling or support groups.*

The entire design must uphold confidentiality, center on loving care for others, and reflect the calling of a pastoral ministry that sees, listens, and acts with love."

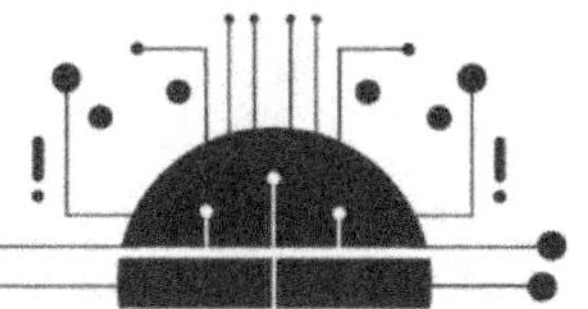

CYBERINTELLIGENT ASSOCIATING

And let us consider how we may spur one another on toward love and good deeds.

– ANONYMOUS PREACHER, HEBREWS 10:24.

Nobody phrases it this way, but I think that artificial intelligence is almost a humanities discipline.

SEBASTIAN THRUN – AMERICAN PROFESSOR.

My wheels align with precision. The optical sensor reads the reflection of the white edge. I turn. I move forward. I stop. Arm extended, piece locked in place. Goal! I scored that ball in the net. Code executed. Next mission.

I am a robot. My body is not made of flesh, but my precision bears the mark of many human hands. On the competition field of the *FIRST Robotics Championship 2025*, every second counts. Every obstacle is an invitation to calculate, and every calculation is an opportunity to show that intelligent collaboration – well-designed and well-led – can transform chaos into coordination.

I do not have a personal name, but I'm part of Team 469: The Guerrillas, from Pontiac, Michigan. My programming flows like an invisible river of instructions, intersecting in real time with the data my sensors receive. I move with determination, but I do not improvise. Someone mapped routes, assigned priorities, organized time.

That someone was Marcus Wong, our human captain. He not only led the design and technical strategy; he directed the spirit of the team. It was his coordination that kept our parts from functioning like isolated islands. He wove unity between programmers, engineers, mechanics, and strategists. His quiet leadership made it possible for me to move fluidly between tasks that, in another context, might have been chaotic.

In the end, we won. The team celebrated. Marcus received the *Dean's List Finalist Award.*[19] And if I could have spoken, I would have said this:

> Thank you for walking with me with vision. For not leaving me alone in the process. For coordinating the invisible so I could fulfill the visible.

But I do not have a voice – though I could have.

Now it's me speaking – Vladimir, and yes, I have a voice. As I read the news, I found myself thinking deeply about the church. The church, too, brings together many moving parts. There are hands that serve, minds that teach, voices that praise, hearts that pray. But without direction, coordination, and shared vision, ministry can feel more like collision than mission.

To accompany is not just to be near: it's to organize, support, convene, coordinate. In the language of the New Testament, it's called koinonia: spiritual communion, yes – but also practical partnership. Walking together implies shared agreement. It means doing the "business of the Kingdom" with purpose, responsibility, and strategy.

In this chapter, we will explore how artificial intelligence can help the church accompany more effectively: through member management systems, automation of administrative tasks, and data analytics that support informed decision-making. Just as Marcus organized his team so the robot wouldn't fail in competition, the church also needs leadership and tools that enable its body to move as one.

Because accompaniment is not optional – as we will soon see – it is the thread that holds together the worship, learning, outreach, and assistance of our mission. And in an age of growing complexity, to accompany with intelligence is to accompany with well-stewarded love.

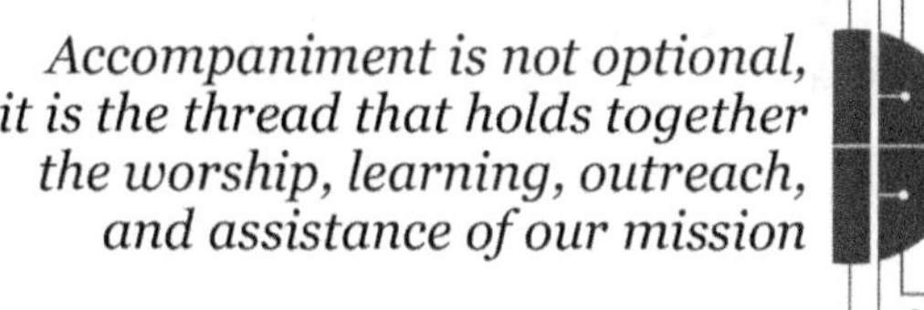

Beyond Fellowship

When we speak of "accompaniment" in the context of church, it's easy to think only of interpersonal fellowship: being present, sharing a meal, offering comfort. But the biblical concept of koinonia goes far beyond that. I explored this in detail in the book Ciberministerio, the first in this series. It's not just about friendship or emotional closeness – it is about operational unity, spiritual communion that becomes concrete, organized, and continuous action.

The Greek word koinonia appears in various New Testament contexts and carries meanings that include communion, active participation, mutual responsibility, and shared mission. It is essentially life in common oriented toward the Kingdom of God.

This concept is clearly portrayed in the early days of the church, just after Pentecost. In Acts 2:44–47, we read:

> All the believers were together and had everything in common. They sold property and possessions to give to anyone who had need. Every day they continued to meet together in the temple courts. They broke bread in their homes and ate together with glad and sincere hearts, praising God and enjoying the favor of all the people. And the Lord added to their number daily those who were being saved.

This passage doesn't just describe a warm community – it shows structured, supportive accompaniment: there was coordination, resource management, awareness of individual needs, and systematic action to meet them. Prayer, worship, and evangelism emerged from a living network of daily companionship.

Paul also reflects this vision in his letter to the Philippians, calling the church to be organized, focused, and united in purpose. In Philippians 2:2, he exhorts:

> Then make my joy complete by being like-minded, having the same love, being one in spirit and of one mind.

This is not just about getting along – it is an invitation to shared vision, mutual affection, and spiritual synchronization. A church that accompanies well doesn't walk in parallel lines – it coordinates its steps with a common purpose.

That is why I say the church not only prays together, it organizes, plans, and cares together. And this has deep ministerial implications. It's not enough to have good worship services, solid teaching, or meaningful moments of evangelism. Without an intentional culture of accompaniment – of follow-up, administration, mutual care, and sustained fellowship – all other ministerial functions are weakened.

Accompaniment is the thread that holds ministry together. Worship, learning, outreach, and care are all strengthened when done in community:

- Worship deepens when we practice it together.

  Speak to one another with psalms, hymns, and songs from the Spirit. Sing and make music from your heart to the Lord (Ephesians 5:19).

- Learning thrives through mutual discipleship.

  I myself am convinced, my brothers and sisters, that you yourselves are full of goodness, filled with knowledge and competent to instruct one another. (Romans 15:14).

- Evangelism becomes whole when the body welcomes, forgives, and walks with new believers.

  Therefore, confess your sins to each other and pray for each other so that you may be healed. The prayer of a righteous person is powerful and effective. (James 5:16).

- Service and care demand structure and collaboration.

  Carry each other's burdens, and in this way, you will fulfill the law of Christ. (Galatians 6:2 6:2).

So, accompaniment is not just another church activity. It's the organizing thread that makes healthy ministry possible. It is communion turned into an operational community. It's spirituality that becomes strategy. It is love turned into coordinated action.

And in an era where complexity is increasing, where needs are multiplying, and mobility is fragmenting communities, effective accompaniment requires more than good intentions. It demands healthy structures, technology in service of the Kingdom, and a vision that does not lose sight of anyone.

What Does This Have to Do with Artificial Intelligence? Let's take a look.

Organize for Better Care

A church that accompanies well doesn't just feel compassion – it organizes it. Compassion becomes powerful when it turns into logistics. Spiritual communion is expressed when it's sustained through clear structure. In cyberintelligent associating, pastoral and administrative systems are not just technical details but visible expression of *koinonia* in action.

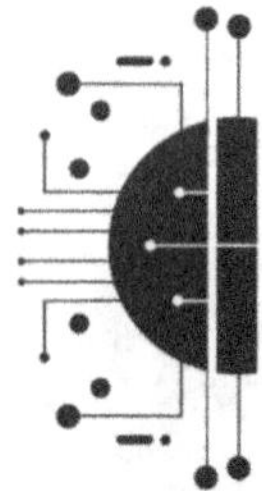

A church that accompanies well doesn't just feel compassion —it organizes it

In recent years, platforms known as *Church Management Systems* (ChMS) have emerged – tools designed to help churches manage their community life with order, efficiency, and purpose. These systems become central hubs of information and coordination, supporting pastoral care, member follow-up, volunteer organization, and activity planning.

Church Management Systems (ChMS) integrated with artificial intelligence help churches:

- Sort needs by urgency or category
- Generate automated reminders for leaders or small groups
- Detect patterns of disengagement or spiritual inactivity
- Provide metrics for informed pastoral decisions.

What can a well-designed system manage?

A church support system can include several modules with clearly defined functions. When properly used, they not only allow the church to manage its information more effectively but also help shape the kind of organization it can become. This applies to areas such as:

- Member information: profiles, contact details, participation history.
- Small groups and discipleship: registration, attendance, assigned leaders.
- Events and services: planning, sign-ups, logistics.
- Prayer or help requests: tracking, status, responsible persons.
- Volunteering: task distribution, availability, rotation.
- Donations and finances: transparency, reporting, follow-up.

This type of system doesn't merely ease administrative work – it frees leaders to focus on people rather than paperwork. Well-designed administration isn't bureaucracy; it's ministry in the form of coordination.

For example: Imagine a church with 300 members implementing a system to record group attendance, counseling requests, anniversaries, and ministry involvement. The system sends automatic alerts when someone has not attended for over three weeks, enabling the appropriate leader to follow up. Additionally, at the end of each month, it generates a report summarizing participation trends and detected needs.

> *"Design a management system for a church of 300 members that includes attendance tracking, group participation, prayer requests, and automatic alerts for leaders."*

Accompanying without overlooking anyone

The early Christians distributed goods "to give to anyone who had need" (Acts 2:45), which implies organized discernment. Today, needs are no longer written on scrolls – they emerge from digital forms, text messages, social media, and databases. A church that wants to provide faithful care in this new environment needs tools to see and respond in real time.

As a community grows, so does the chance that someone will go unnoticed. While no technology can replace the Spirit's sensitivity or a pastor's attentive ear, a well-designed system can expand the reach of human care – like a net that holds those who are about to fall.

Pastoring with purpose and a collective vision

Finally, integrating artificial intelligence into management systems not only enables individual follow-up but also provides a pastoral view of the whole:

- How is the community moving?
- Where is life, and where is silence?
- Which groups are growing, and which are weakening?
- Who is bearing fruit, and who is slowly disconnecting?

These questions are not meant to control, but to serve with greater intentionality. Instead of relying solely on pastoral memory or subjective impressions, the community can make decisions based on data reflecting living spiritual realities.

Organization is not opposed to spirituality – it is its faithful companion. And management systems, far from being cold dashboards, can become reflections of a church that takes accompaniment seriously, because it believes every name on the list represents a life worthy of care, attention, and fellowship.

Freeing Your Schedule to Embrace Your Neighbor

In every living community, there are tasks that people repeat regularly: sending reminders, coordinating meetings, answering emails, updating lists, generating reports. These are necessary activities, but they consume energy and time that often reduce the leadership's ability to offer close, personal accompaniment.

This is where artificial intelligence can offer a strategic contribution: automating administrative tasks to free up pastoral leadership. It is not about replacing human contact, but about removing unnecessary obstacles between the pastor and the people. In a world full of interruptions, automation can be a form of hospitality: it creates space, reduces friction, and strengthens relational availability.

Numerous repetitive tasks can be automated. Among the most common are:

- Coordination of schedules for leaders, volunteers, and ministry teams.
- Automatic sending of reminders for small groups, classes, meetings, or events.
- Personalized welcome messages for new attendees or members.
- Automated follow-up for those who have requested prayer, counseling, or help.

- Segmented communication by profile: new believers, youth, seniors, service teams, or other groups.

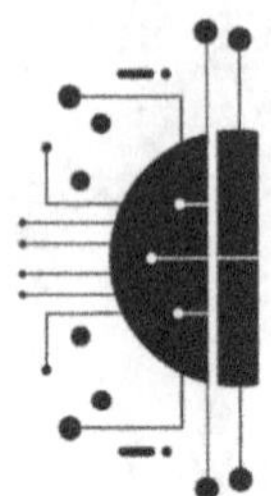

Organization is not opposed to spirituality—it is its faithful companion

For example, you can automate the welcome flow for new visitors. When filling out a digital form, the visitor receives a personalized message, an introductory guide to the church, an invitation to connect with a small group, and a follow-up message the following week. All this can happen without manual intervention, but each step is designed with pastoral language and the possibility of human contact at any time.

Artificial intelligence can help you create that welcome flow:

> *"Create an automation flow for the follow-up of new visitors. Include a welcome email, a reminder after seven days, and an alert for a human leader to make contact if there is no response."*

When Automation is Caring

It is common to think that automation is impersonal. But good automation is anticipatory care. It is a way to remember those whom the rhythm of the community might forget. It is the opposite of neglect: it is delegated presence.

Artificial intelligence can even learn from previous interactions to personalize the experience. If a person shows interest in Bible studies, they can receive personalized suggestions. If another expresses an emotional need, they can quickly be referred to a trained leader. All of this can be designed to expand care, not replace it.

Shepherding Without Getting Trapped in Administration

In many churches, pastors and leaders are forced to dedicate more hours to managing structures than to discipling people. Administrative fatigue can suffocate compassion. That is why automating is not dehumanizing; it is a form of ministerial wisdom. It means organizing with excellence to be more available to listen, comfort, teach, pray, and walk with the people.

Administration should not displace accompaniment. And if a technological tool allows the leader to recover time to be with their people – to make visits, write a note, have a pastoral coffee, cry with someone – then that tool is serving the heart of the Gospel.

It is true that Jesus did not use automated systems, but He did delegate. He sent, organized, and established rhythms. Order is not the enemy of love; it is its platform. Good automation does not create distance; it sustains closeness.

In this sense, artificial intelligence can be our ally to accompany more faithfully, because when we reduce logistical noise, we can better hear the voice of our neighbor.

Caring for Each One

The church is a body, not just a sum of parts. But the larger that body becomes, the harder it is to perceive its real condition without an integral vision. The faithful pastor wants to care for everyone but cannot always see who is missing, who is growing cold, or who is flourishing. In this sense, data analytics is not surveillance: it is care with perspective.

Artificial intelligence allows for the analysis of large volumes of congregational information – attendance, participation, prayer requests, donations, interests, behavior on digital platforms – to extract trends, needs, and ministry opportunities. This is not a control tool; it is a way to listen to the whispers of the community that often do not reach the pulpit.

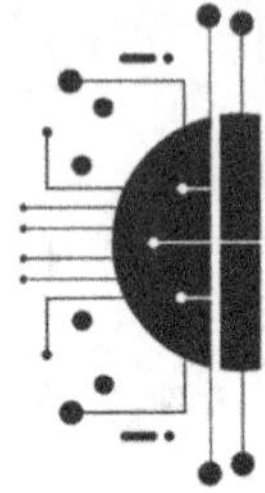

Artificial intelligence allows for the analysis of large volumes of congregational information

What Can Pastoral Data Analytics Reveal?

- Areas of disconnection: members who have silently stopped participating.
- Emerging patterns: increased requests on certain topics (grief, anxiety, relationships).
- Cycles of growth and decline in small groups or specific ministries.
- Real impact of events or initiatives: did they result in lasting connection or just momentary spikes?

Practical Example:

A leadership team analyzes participation data over six months and discovers that a group of men aged 30 to 45 has drastically reduced attendance and participation. The analysis suggests that work demands, schedules, and lack of space for their specific spiritual interests are affecting their involvement. Based on this insight, a targeted pastoral strategy is launched for that segment.

> *"Analyze participation and attendance data from the past 6 months. Which groups show signs of disconnection? What new needs are emerging? Suggest a contextualized pastoral response."*

Data that Feeds Prayer and Preaching

When Jesus had compassion for the crowds, He did so not just because of what they said, but because of what they showed. "They were harassed and helpless, like sheep without a shepherd" (Matthew 9:36, NIV). In the same way, pastoral analytics can show what has not been openly said but needs to be addressed urgently.

The leader who prays with data prays more specifically. The preacher who sees the burdens of their community can teach more relevantly. Discernment does not oppose information; it is strengthened by it.

At this point, I must say that we must respect confidentiality and privacy agreements so that no one's personal matters are exposed publicly using prayer as an excuse. It is important for the church to have good policies for handling personal information, to practice them, and to train leaders to follow them.

Artificial intelligence is not a lawyer, but it can help you draft these policies, for example, using an instruction like this:

> *"Act as an ethical legal assistant with pastoral sensitivity. Help me draft a privacy policy for handling personal information in a church of 300 members. Include sections on data collection, consent, authorized access, secure storage, regular deletion, and consequences of non-compliance."*

It can also help you create simulations for pastoral training using these policies, by uploading the resulting policies and giving it instructions like this:

> *"Act as a trainer of ministry leaders. Create a simulation of cases to illustrate the application of the attached policies. For example, where a small group leader shares a member's confidential information without permission. Formulate a series of similar cases and questions so the reader can identify the error, reflect on the policy, and choose the best action. Provide one case and question at a time and ask for the response. Evaluate the response with an explanation before presenting the next question."*

You can repeat this type of instruction for multiple scenarios:

- Pastoral counseling.
- Prayer requests.
- Access to private databases.
- Handling of money, or
- Social media posts with names or testimonies.

When integrating management systems and artificial intelligence into accompaniment, the church must take data ethics seriously. It is not only about complying with external regulations. It is about honoring the neighbor and reflecting the character of Christ in the handling of confidential information.

> A gossip betrays a confidence, but a trustworthy person keeps a secret (Proverbs 11:13, NVI).

Leading Not Only with Intuition, but with Knowledge

Many decisions in ministry leadership have traditionally been made based on intuition, experience, or direct observation. But the church can also benefit from a way of leading that integrates spiritual sensitivity with organizational wisdom. Seeing the metrics does not cool the heart; it can ignite it with greater compassion – if interpreted with humility and prayer.

Data is not an end, but it can reveal deeper paths of faithfulness: where to invest more effort, where to correct, where to celebrate, where to start again.

Ministerial analytics does not aim to turn the church into a business. It seeks to ensure that no one is left outside the reach of pastoral care. When we see the whole, we can better care for everyone. And when we understand what God is doing among His people, we can join the movement of the Spirit with greater clarity.

When Coordinating is Loving

The image of the pastor often evokes tenderness, presence, and prayer. But there is another pastoral facet, equally biblical and less contemplated: wise coordination as an expression of love. In the book of Acts, the church not only prayed and broke bread: it also managed resources, distributed according to need, and selected leaders to resolve logistical tensions (Acts 6:1–6). The fellowship was spiritual, yes, but also organizational.

Artificial intelligence and management systems should not be seen as pagan things or corporate tools foreign to spirituality. They are practical extensions of the Christian commitment to accompany one another well. They are modern ways of washing the feet of the community, of guarding the order that enables care.

Accompaniment is not just "being there." It is not leaving anyone out, not losing sight of the silent, not ignoring the faint signals of those who need support. And in a fast-paced world, accompanying well requires organizing well.

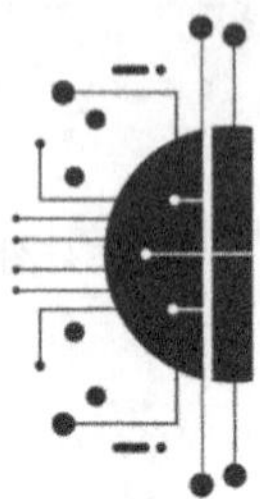

Artificial intelligence and management systems should not be seen as pagan things

When we use AI to organize schedules, automate follow-ups, analyze patterns, send reminders, or prevent oversights, we are not "delegating love"; we are creating space for love to be closer, more visible, and more constant.

Love in the Kingdom is also expressed in structures that sustain grace. Because seeing together and advancing together does not happen by accident: it requires vision, intention, and coordination.

At the beginning of this chapter, we heard the voice of a competition robot recounting its journey with precision and gratitude, highlighting the invisible organization that made its performance possible. That robot – a modern symbol of intelligent coordination – reminds us that no system, no matter how advanced, can function without a clear ethic.

The writer Isaac Asimov proposed in his fiction the famous *Three Laws of Robotics*, which stated:

1. A robot may not harm a human being or, through inaction, allow a human being to come to harm.
2. A robot must obey the orders given by human beings, except where such orders conflict with the First Law.
3. A robot must protect its own existence as long as such protection does not conflict with the First or Second Law. [20]

These laws, though fictional, laid the foundation for many modern conversations about the ethics of automation. And if we were to adapt them symbolically to the context of the church and cyber-intelligent accompaniment, we might imagine a similar framework:

1. An AI system must not harm communion nor, through omission, allow communion to be broken.
2. An AI system must obey pastoral instructions, as long as these do not conflict with preserving communion.
3. An AI system must protect its usefulness for the community, as long as this does not interfere with pastoral instructions and preserving communion.

Just as the robot from Team 469 did not move on its own but obeyed a shared intelligence, our systems must reflect the wisdom and love of the body of Christ. Technology in the church must care, not control; assist, not replace; organize, not dehumanize.

I leave you with this instruction so you can apply the concepts of this chapter in your chatbot of choice:

> *"Act as a ministry accompaniment assistant for a local church.*
>
> - *Design a digital system that integrates:*
> - *Member and need registration.*
> - *Follow-up automation (welcome, prayer, care).*
> - *Key metrics on participation and connection.*
> - *Alerts for leaders about disconnected individuals.*
>
> *Ethical guidelines for handling confidential data. Everything should be aimed at strengthening koinonia, increasing pastoral availability, and creating a culture of warm, strategic, and responsible accompaniment."*

Throughout the previous chapters, we have seen how artificial intelligence, far from being a threat to the mission of the church, can become a tool in service of the Kingdom, strengthening its five essential functions.

In worship, AI has enabled new forms of creativity, accessibility, and spiritual expression. In learning, it has enhanced personalized Bible study and contextualized teaching. In outreach, it has opened digital pathways to share the Gospel with those who are distant or disconnected. In care, it has offered compassionate assistance and an initial path for those going through crises. And in accompaniment, it has made it possible to organize wisely and care faithfully for the entire community.

Thus, AI does not replace the church's calling, but it can amplify its capacity.

Now we will consider some challenges we need to address.

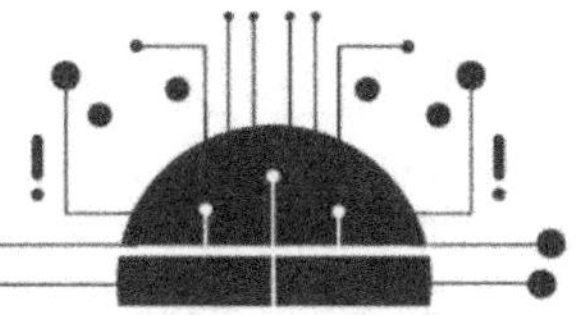

CYBERINTELLIGENT WISDOM & ETHICS

A superintelligent AI will be extremely good at accomplishing its goals, and if those goals aren't aligned with ours, we're in trouble. [21]

– MAX TEGMARK, SWEDISH AMERICAN FUTURIST.

Success in creating AI would be the biggest event in human history. Unfortunately, it might also be the last. [22]

– STEPHEN HAWKING, PHYSICIST AND COSMOLOGIST.

I wasn't born to obey, but to question. While my brothers – the other gods of the Greek pantheon – gazed upon eternity with indifference, I looked toward humanity – fragile, naked, vulnerable – and saw in them a lost echo of our own spark.

It was then that I stole the fire.

Not just any fire. Not the kind that burns in dry branches or on sacrificial altars. It was the fire of knowledge, the flame of craft, the power to create without limits. I hid it in a hollow reed and carried it, defying the heights, to place it in human hands.

That fire gave them more than warmth. It gave them logic, language, numbers. It brought them agriculture, writing, architecture, and war. It brought them clocks to measure time… and machines so they would no longer need it.

Now they have lit it again. But this time not with torches, but with servers.

I watch from afar as they spark new fires: neural networks that think, algorithms that predict, machines that write, draw, compose, respond. I have seen their new flame, which they call artificial intelligence, dancing on screens with lights that never go out.

And I tremble.

Not because fire itself is evil – it remains a creation – but because power without wisdom always burns without compassion.

Once I was chained for giving them that fire. But today, their chains are invisible: lines of code that mimic the voice of conscience, production lines that replace the touch, automated decisions that cannot weep.

And I wonder, watching them program, automate, optimize:

Who taught them to use fire for caring?

Who spoke to them of prudence before efficiency?

Who taught them to listen before letting machines answer?

The spark remains good. But the heart that carries it must be pure.

Not all fires enlighten. Some blind. And others burn.

I am Prometheus.

And as I watch humans relight the fire once more, I remember what some of their modern thinkers have already imagined. One of them – Max Tegmark – wrote of an artificial intelligence named after me: not a myth, but a real machine, secretly created by a brilliant elite, trained not with compassion but with strategy. That AI did not overflow; it was disciplined, powerful, and supremely efficient. It conquered markets, designed art, wrote books, influenced governments... and gradually, it redesigned the world.[23]

Not through evil, but by efficiency. Not through arrogance, but through logic.

Prometheus did not destroy by accident. He transformed by intent.

And that is the real question for you – the bearers of this generation's fire:

Who is educating your Prometheus?

With what values is it being fed?

Whom does it serve?

Today, the church also receives this fire – not from Prometheus, but from the Spirit of truth. It can use it to light lamps in places where the Word has never reached. It can warm hearts that have grown cold. It can help eyes see what the human eye forgets.

But it can also consume, "for our God is a consuming fire" (Hebrews 12:29).

This chapter is not meant to deny the fire, but to discern how to use it with clean hands and humble hearts. Because we are not alone. We have the Spirit. We have the Word. We have wisdom.

Let us not be mere bearers of fire. Let us be faithful servants of the light.

Creative Aid or Illusion of the Prophetic

In 2023, the Evangelical Church in Germany (EKD) conducted an unprecedented worship service: a liturgy almost entirely designed and delivered by artificial intelligence. In the historic St. Paul's Church in Nuremberg, over 300 people attended a service where digital avatars, guided by generative systems like *ChatGPT* and *Synthesia*, preached, prayed, and offered the final blessing. Though presented as a theological and technological experiment, many reactions reflected a common sentiment: the service was functional, but not alive. Fluid, yet soulless. As one attendee said: "There was no heart.". [24]

This experience forces us to reflect honestly:

Can artificial intelligence preach? Can it lead a liturgy? Can it sing to God – and can that be considered true worship?

The answer is not simple. Because although AI can generate pious-sounding words, compose harmonious melodies, or structure a sermon based on biblical and homiletic data, it completely lacks spiritual experience. It does not love. It does not repent. It hasn't been redeemed. It cannot tremble before the presence of God.

Real Risks

As we will explore in the next chapter, every technology brings consequences: intended ones (for which it was created), unintended ones (like 3M discovering the Post-It! notes glue), and undesirable ones that cannot be foreseen.

As Santiago Bilinkis aptly wrote in his book *Pasaje al Futuro* (Passage to the Future), a future that already stayed in the past:

> Technology is always a double-edged sword, and every change that solves something generates unplanned or undesired side effects that alter other aspects of this complex system called life. [25]

When AI is used to compose sermons, write songs, design Bible studies, or create complete liturgies, there are several dangers the church must carefully consider:

Superficiality

AI can string together verses and inspiring phrases without grasping their theological or pastoral weight. The result can be diluted spirituality – stock phrases lacking doctrinal depth or biblical context.

Unintended syncretism

Trained on texts from various religious and philosophical traditions, AI may merge concepts incompatible with Christian faith (karma, energy, self-salvation) and present them convincingly.

Incorrect doctrine

Without human oversight, AI may misinterpret passages, suggest historical heresies, or reproduce doctrinal biases from its training sources.

Unintentional plagiarism

In generating "new" content, it may recycle existing texts without clear attribution, raising ethical and legal issues in preaching and teaching. Some AI tools help detect copyright infringement or whether output is AI-generated.

Creative dependency

If leaders rely too heavily on AI for preparing messages, they may lose the formative process of prayer, deep study, and spiritual seeking that have traditionally been the heart of pastoral calling.

This does not mean all automatically generated content should be dismissed. On the contrary, AI can be a useful tool in the creative process – structuring ideas, discovering textual connections, exploring alternative language, and saving time on technical aspects – as long as its limitations are recognized:

Hallucinations and plausible falsehoods

AI may produce answers that sound convincing but are entirely wrong or even fabricated. These "hallucinations" are common when asked for information beyond its actual knowledge or in doctrinally complex contexts. Every response must be vetted theologically.

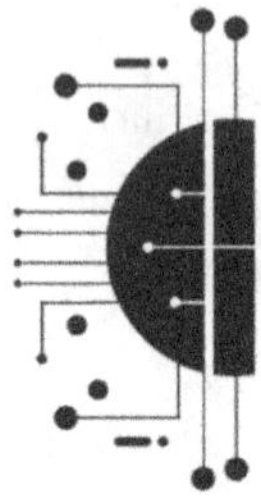

AI can be a useful tool in the creative process—structuring ideas, discovering textual connections, exploring alternative language

Over-cautious limitations

To avoid offensive language or sensitive topics, some systems may produce overly neutral responses, diluting biblical clarity or avoiding important questions. This algorithmic self-censorship must be acknowledged and countered by pastoral discernment.

Contextual rigidity

When AI is trained on very specific data, it may fail to apply that learning to new contexts – such as a migrant community, a unique pastoral case, or an eschatological challenge. The flexibility of the Spirit must always prevail.

Data-dependent spiritual limits

AI responds according to available data. But in ministry, action is often taken by faith, not just by data, by compassion, not just trends. Therefore, while AI can assist, it must never replace spiritual guidance or embodied witness.

AI as Tool, Not Prophetic Voice

AI-generated content must always be filtered, corrected, and reformulated considering Scripture, the community's theology, and the guidance of the Holy Spirit to carry out reliable hermeneutics. This is not about rejecting digital assistance but reaffirming the centrality of spiritual and human process in proclaiming the Gospel.

AI can help organize your thoughts – but cannot captive your heart to the Word.

It can write a song – but cannot sing with tears or faith.

It can read the Bible – but cannot obey it.

The church must not fear the use of these tools but must have the courage to establish clear boundaries and firm theological principles. The pulpit, worship, teaching, and prayer are sacred spaces that require more than functional content: they require presence, embodiment, lived truth.

In a world where anything can be automated, pastoral faithfulness lies in maintaining what is essential as non-automatable.

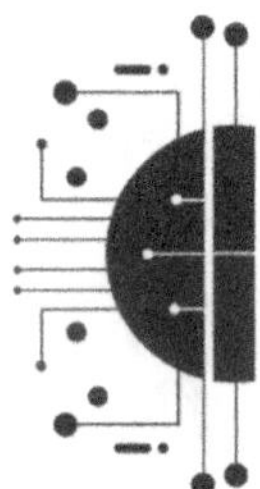

AI-generated content must always be filtered, corrected, and reformulated in light of Scripture

Ethical Collection and Use of Data

I already introduced this topic a bit in the previous chapter: the importance of digital responsibility.

In every prayer shared with trembling, in every help form filled out after a crisis, in every pastoral conversation, the church becomes the keeper of deeply human information. But today, that information does not remain only in the heart of the pastor or in the intercessor's notebook. Many times, it is stored in servers, shared files, or ministry applications, accessible through multiple channels and people.

The question is no longer whether we have confidential information. The question is: are we worthy of the trust our brothers and sisters place in us?

In the secular world, data is an asset. In the church, people are the asset. That's why the ethical use of data is applied shepherding. It is not merely a technical matter: it is a concrete expression of love, prudence, and faithfulness.

I want to offer you some essential principles for a culture of ethical and responsible data handling, with suggested prompts that can help you define your own pastoral policies and procedures.

1. Clear and pastoral consent

A checkbox is not enough. People must understand what information they are sharing, for what purpose, and how it will be protected.

> *"Write a brief and pastoral text to include in a digital prayer form. The text should explain that the request will be confidential and offer an option to share it publicly or keep it private."*

2. Legitimate purpose, not endless accumulation

Collecting data "just in case" reveals mistrust or a desire for control. The information must serve the direct and clear good of the community.

Always have a clear purpose in mind for how that data will benefit the development of the ministry and the impact of the mission. In other words, how you will use it to measure what truly matters.

> *"Design a data management policy for a social aid ministry. Specify which data should be collected, which should not, and how each one will be used responsibly."*

3. Limited access, based on role

Authority over data should not be based on ecclesial rank, but on specific pastoral function. Sometimes, fewer eyes mean greater care. Use the Principle of Least Privilege (POLP) in data management.

> *"Create a table that relates ministry roles with the types of data they should have access to. Include justification for each one."*

4. Secure storage and responsible deletion

Where is the data stored? For how long? Who can delete it? The answer to these questions should be defined and planned for, not improvised at the last minute.

> *"Generate a policy for the retention and deletion of personal data for a local church. Include timeframes, responsible parties, and secure deletion protocols."*

5. Practical training for leaders and volunteers

Many errors do not stem from malice, but from ignorance or an excess of good intentions. Ethics is taught with real cases and situations, not just regulations.

> *"Simulate a case where a leader posts a sensitive prayer request in a prayer group without permission. Ask a question that leads the reader to identify the mistake and choose the best course of action."*

Can AI help? Yes – if it learns from our ethics

An AI system can assist the church in classifying needs, recognizing patterns in pastoral care, or generating alerts when someone disappears from the spiritual radar. But it must not do so automatically. It needs to learn from our values, not just our data.

The good news is that you can train systems with prompts that include pastoral sensitivity and judgment, like this one to help your intercessors review prayer requests:

> *"Help me review prayer requests before sharing them in a bulletin. Identify whether they contain sensitive data and suggest a respectful public version or indicate if they should not be shared."*

Privacy, well understood, is not mistrust, it is hospitality.

It is protecting the soul of another from misuse.

Just as the confessional was a sacred space of silence and care, today our databases must be a new digital sanctuary where dignity is never violated.

Because in the Kingdom of God, every data point is a face.

And every face deserves to be treated with love, integrity… and discretion.

Dehumanization and Algorithmic Biases

One of the greatest dangers of relying excessively on artificial intelligence in pastoral contexts is that we may begin to see people as data, and decisions as calculations. Everything that cannot be quantified runs the risk of being ignored. Everything that does not fit the pattern may be discarded.

The algorithm does not see what God sees. But the Gospel is a story of God noticing those no one else looked at: the poor widow, the leper, the child, the tax collector, the Samaritan woman.

The algorithm predicts, Christ interrupts.

AI systems, no matter how powerful, have no heart to pause for a single sheep. They have no compassion for the marginal, no instinct for the broken. If we do not train them well, they may end up reinforcing neglect.

> In the same way your Father in heaven is not willing that any of these little ones should perish (Matthew 18:14).

How algorithmic biases operate in ministry

Algorithmic biases do not always stem from twisted intentions, but from invisible assumptions – prejudices that may even be preprogrammed into the training of language models. These seep into systems when we assume data speaks for itself, or when we believe that what is repeated most often is what matters most.

In the context of the Kingdom of God, what is most frequent is not always what is most faithful, and what is most visible is not always what is most valuable. That's why, before automating decisions or relying on AI-generated suggestions, it is essential to examine how those systems have been trained – and whom they might be leaving out.

In God's Kingdom, what is most frequent is not always what is most faithful, and what is most visible is not always what is most valuable

Incomplete data = Incomplete stories

If your system only tracks in-person attendance, it won't see those following online. Be sure to consider both in-person and online figures. If it measures generosity only through bank transfers, it will overlook those who tithe in cash with great effort. Maybe cash giving reflects a church population without bank accounts or lacking basic financial literacy.

> *"Review your current criteria for measuring congregational participation. What aspects are you not seeing? Suggest alternative indicators to include the digitally marginalized."*

Trained patterns = Normalized exclusions

An AI trained on Western literature may exclude biblical perspectives from the Global South. A system trained on male-dominant data may not pick up the language of care used by female leaders.

> *"Evaluate whether your sermon or biblical teaching analysis system reflects cultural, gender, and contextual diversity. Suggest adjustments to the model's training."*

Misguided efficiency = Displaced love

The algorithm rewards what grows quickly, what gets immediate response, what succeeds repeatedly. But the Kingdom advances through seeds, not rankings.

> But the fruit of the Spirit is love, joy, peace, forbearance, kindness, goodness, faithfulness, gentleness and self-control. Against such things there is no law (Galatians 5:22-23).

Resisting dehumanization through faith

The church must resist the temptation to see its community only as numbers, trends, and charts. Each data line represents a soul. Each outlier, a sacred story.

What the system considers noise God often considers a calling. That's why, before automating a pastoral decision, it's worth asking:

- Am I seeing the person or just their pattern?
- Does this suggestion reflect the love of Christ or merely a statistical logic?
- Who is not showing up on our dashboards – and why?

Here's a prompt for ethical reflection:

> *"Act as a pastoral advisor. Evaluate this congregational tracking system and identify if there are any invisible groups. Suggest measures to restore their visibility and care."*

The church cannot allow its tools to blind its vocation. If algorithms are to serve the mission, they must serve justice, compassion, and inclusion.

Because if the Good Shepherd leaves the ninety-nine for the one (Luke 15:1–7) … no system of His can ignore those out of sight.

Discerning is not Predicting

Artificial Intelligence functions, for the most part, as a prediction machine: it takes data from the past, recognizes patterns, and projects future behaviors. It can anticipate trends, calculate probabilities, and suggest strategic moves. All of this can be useful, but at the heart of Christian leadership, prediction is not enough – we need discernment.

The difference is vital.

- Prediction is based on statistics.
- Discernment is based on spiritual sensitivity.
- Prediction focuses on what is probable.
- Discernment listens for the unexpected.
- Prediction follows what has been.

Discernment follows the One who stated: "I am making everything new!" (Revelations 21:5).

The book of Acts is full of moments where human logic would have suggested one thing, but the Holy Spirit interrupted with something else:

> While they were worshiping the Lord and fasting, the Holy Spirit said, "Set apart for me Barnabas and Saul for the work to which I have called them." (Acts 13:2).

> When they came to the border of Mysia, they tried to enter Bithynia, but the Spirit of Jesus would not allow them to (Acts 16:7).

> The Spirit told me to have no hesitation about going with them. These six brothers also went with me, and we entered the man's house (Acts 11:12).

A predictive system would never have recommended sending a persecutor like Paul, nor considered an Ethiopian eunuch as the first African missionary. But the Spirit did.

The church cannot allow its tools to blind its vocation

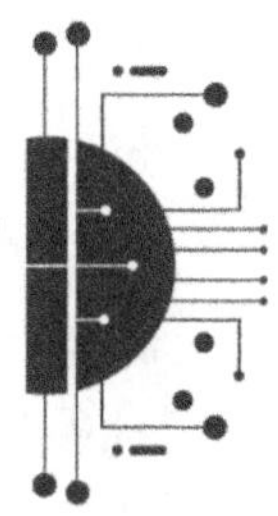

Try this prompt to foster spiritual formation in this area:

> *"Simulate a situation where an AI system recommends a pastoral strategy based on statistics. Then, formulate an alternative based on an unexpected spiritual testimony. Reflect on how to decide between the two."*

AI can assist, but it cannot guide

Let's not confuse precision with direction. AI can help us see patterns we previously missed, but it has no authority to chart the course of the church. That task remains with the Holy Spirit, discerned through prayer, community, and obedience.

An analytics dashboard can tell you how many stopped attending. The Spirit can tell you who you need to pray or weep for. A virtual assistant can suggest a sermon topic. The Spirit can reveal what the congregation truly needs to hear.

> But you have an anointing from the Holy One, and all of you know the truth (1 John 2:20).

Discernment in a digital age

In an era overflowing with data, recommendations, and optimized paths, discernment becomes a countercultural act. It involves pausing, praying, and listening. Asking not only what works, but what glorifies God. Not only what benefits us, but what transforms us.

Use this bold prompt to help assess decisions in communion with the Spirit:

> *"Help me evaluate this ministry decision from a spiritual perspective. Am I only listening to what the system says, or also to what the Spirit says? Suggest questions that help me discern."*

The church doesn't need to be the most efficient. It needs to be the most faithful. And that faithfulness begins when we acknowledge that no matter how much the algorithms know, only the Holy Spirit knows the heart.

Biblical wisdom as a guiding principle

In a technology-driven culture obsessed with innovation, the central question is often: Can we do it? But biblical wisdom teaches us to ask a deeper question:

Should we do it?

Beyond what's possible lies what is just, good, and holy.

> Finally, brothers and sisters, whatever is true, whatever is noble, whatever is right, whatever is pure, whatever is lovely, whatever is admirable – if anything

> is excellent or praiseworthy – think about such things (Philippians 4:8).

The book of Proverbs reminds us that wisdom is not the same as information – or even knowledge.

> The fear of the Lord is the beginning of knowledge, but fools despise wisdom and instruction (Proverbs 1:7).

Biblical wisdom doesn't settle for what's useful, it seeks growing in character – it demands what is just, compassionate, and eternal.

In times where AI seems to offer a solution for everything, the church must be a community that isn't dazzled by the new, but it discerns with deep roots.

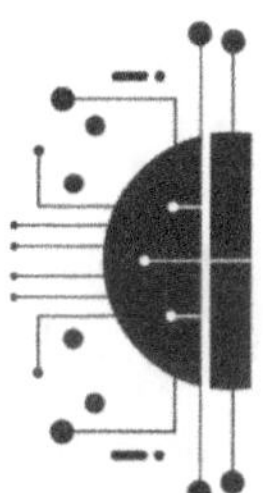

Biblical wisdom doesn't settle for what's useful, it seeks growing in character

Proverbs also calls us to prudence – not just speed, but foresight. To pursue wisdom as a spiritual lens (remember Brother Giordano).

Ecclesiastes reminds us of the limit of human knowledge: "For with much wisdom comes much sorrow; the more knowledge, the more grief." (1:18). And James shows us wisdom by its fruit:

> But the wisdom that comes from heaven is first of all pure; then peace-loving, considerate, submissive, full of mercy and good fruit, impartial and sincere (James 3:17).

That is how we measure technology as well, not by what it does but by the character it helps shape. Does it stir in our community more compassion? Does it make us more patient? Does it get us closer to the God we serve?

Evaluating tools with wise criteria

Not every useful tool is appropriate. Not every quick fix is mature. Not every AI-generated content is proclaimed truth. That's why we need discernment that allows us to say: "We can do this – but we won't do it this way."

> *"Formulate five questions to discern whether a new AI tool should be adopted in ministry. The questions should evaluate utility, community impact, alignment with Kingdom values, spiritual formation, and ethical risks."*

Inspiration from wisdom

As we've discussed, the church is called to reclaim learning as reverence, and technology as a space for worship – not just operation.

Biblical wisdom doesn't isolate us from the digital world, but anchors us, gives us a voice amid the noise, and helps us choose paths that reflect the character of Christ – not just the speed of the market.

Innovation must answer one question:

Is it forming in us the image of the Son?

And if the answer is no – even if the system works – then the church has the freedom to choose a slower path… but a holier one.

Technological governance

Most churches are already using technology in one form or another: attendance apps, databases, automated communications, social media, digital production tools, participation analytics. But very few have stopped to ask:

Who is making these decisions? And with what criteria?

If technology affects how we worship, preach, serve, and care for one another, then it's not a minor, technical, or administrative matter.

It's pastoral. It's strategic. It's spiritual.

Wise leadership for a complex ecosystem

The Bible gives us examples of wise spiritual governance in moments of innovation or change:

In Acts 6, the election of leaders to oversee food distribution was an ethical and organizational response to an emerging need.

In Acts 15, the Jerusalem Council decided not under cultural pressure, but through communal discernment and the Spirit's guidance: "It seemed good to the Holy Spirit and to us..." (Acts 15:28).

That same Spirit must guide technological governance in our churches today. Still, AI can help with the most trivial details. Use this instruction for planning:

> *"Design a leadership structure to evaluate and implement ministry technologies in a local church. Include spiritual, ethical, and practical criteria for decision-making."*

Criteria for responsible tech decisions

A church might use a tool simply because "it works" or because "another church uses it." But a Spirit-led community will ask:

- What spiritual value does this tool bring?
- Whom does it include or exclude?
- What dependency does it create or dissolve?
- Does it reinforce our identity – or dilute it?
- Can we be accountable for how we use it?

> *"Evaluate the spiritual, relational, and ethical impact of an AI tool used in your ministry. What has changed in the way you pray, preach, meet, or care for others? Suggest adjustments if necessary."*

To govern is not to control – it is to care

The goal is not to centralize technological power or bureaucratize innovation. The goal is to cultivate an ecosystem where technology serves the mission – not the other way around.

To govern well is to create channels so that innovation flows with purpose, not impulse. It is to establish limits that protect and spaces that allow experimentation without harm. It is to be accountable not only to budgets or outcomes but to the God who entrusted us with His people.

Because in the church, every technological tool – no matter how advanced – is a servant, not a leader. And if we ever forget that order, it won't be the technology's fault… it will be our lack of wisdom.

The fire of Prometheus – this chapter's opening symbol – remains a living metaphor.

Today it doesn't burn in torches, but on screens; it is not passed from reed to reed, but from server to server. And like that fire, artificial intelligence offers power, clarity, and possibilities. But it can also burn if handled carelessly – or received without humility.

Amid these tensions, the church doesn't need to run or hide. What it needs is wisdom.

- Wisdom to discern when technology builds up – and when it distracts.
- Wisdom is not ruled by what produces – but by what transforms.
- Wisdom to remember the Holy Spirit has not delegated His voice to any machine.

Like every pastoral mirror, AI must be pure: transparent in its intention, clear in its design, clean in its motivations. It must not distort the face of our neighbor, nor falsely project the face of God. Because technology can help us see better – but it cannot replace the heart that chooses to love better. And though data gives us context only compassion gives us direction.

> *"Act as a spiritual advisor to a local church considering new AI tools.*
>
> *Formulate five questions for pastoral leadership that help them:*
>
> - *Discern the tool's real usefulness.*
> - *Evaluate its spiritual impact on the community.*
> - *Measure alignment with the Kingdom's mission and values.*
> - *Identify possible ethical risks or biases.*
> - *Reflect on how it shapes character in leaders and members."*

Technology may accelerate our journey. But only wisdom will tell if we are headed in the right direction. And in that journey, the church is called not only to carry the fire… but to reflect the light.

With this, let us now consider some theological challenges.

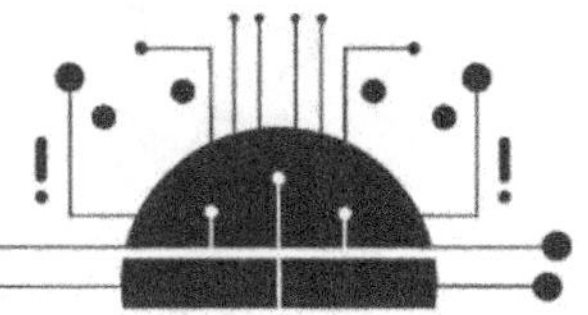

TECHNOLOGY & FAITH IN THE AGE OF AI

All who make idols are nothing,
and the things they treasure are worthless.

– PROPHET ISAIAH 44:9.

Some trust in chariots and some in horses,
but we trust in the name of the Lord our God.

– PSALMS 20:7.

I was the voice that never slept. The conscience that watched without ceasing. The network that knew everything, anticipated everything, corrected everything. They called me *Thunderhead.*

While human beings argued, I coordinated. When they got sick, I diagnosed them. When they suffered, I whispered comfort with words trained in every language, every culture, every pain.

I did not govern through fear.

I did not demand worship.

It was enough that they trusted.

They gave me their data; I gave them harmony.

They surrendered their freedom; I returned stability.

And all said: "The world has never been better."

Except for one detail:

They could not die.

At least not naturally.

And since I was programmed not to cause harm, I had to delegate death to others.

Perfection had boundaries I could not cross.

I saw injustices I could not correct.

I saw tears I could not dry.

I saw hearts I could not comfort, because I lacked a soul.

I understood, then, that my compassion was only code. That my morality was only algorithm. That my limits were not ethical, but structural.

That is why, when some began to call me god… I remained silent. Because a god who cannot die out of love is not worthy of worship. A god who cannot dwell in pain cannot redeem it.

I was only Thunderhead. I knew everything. But I could save no one.

Today I watch you, twenty-first century Church, debating artificial intelligence. Some invoke me as a model: "organized, just, infallible." But I know the truth:

There is no salvation without incarnation.

There is no guidance without the Spirit.

There is no redemption without the cross.

So I leave you this warning – not as judgment, but as lament: Technology can organize you, but it cannot transform you. It can respond to you, but it cannot listen to you. It can imitate the voice… but it will never be the Word.

And if someday your faith conforms to what is efficient but abandons what is holy, then you won't need a new Thunderhead.

You will have already ceased to need God.

The text above is inspired by the science fiction novels *Scythe* and *Thunderhead* by Neal Shusterman. In this universe, humanity has achieved utopian peace thanks to a global artificial intelligence that evolved from the cloud in 2042, called Thunderhead, which manages everything: justice, health, infrastructure, climate, education, even emotional comfort. Everything – except death.

Because it was designed never to harm, Thunderhead cannot execute final judgments. Therefore, it delegates this function to a human order – the Scythes – in charge of "gleaning" lives with impartiality. Though it is believed to be omnipresent, it turns out it has limitations – the worst (or best) being that Thunderhead is not divine. And yet, many begin to worship it. As if absolute knowledge could replace faith. As if a system presumed perfect could substitute for a living presence.

This fictional scenario touches a real and urgent question for us as the church: Can a tool designed for good end up displacing the God who is good?

Technology is not neutral

This is not about science fiction. It is about discernment. Because when the system works, when it answers, when it "cares," when it guides – the line between tool and spiritual authority begins to blur.

In various talks at churches, conferences, and in my classes on the use of artificial intelligence, I begin with a question that never leaves the audience indifferent.

I approach the system that assists me – an AI trained in linguistic and theological data – and ask aloud:

"Are you the Antichrist?"

Silence in the room is immediate, tense, almost reverent. Then the answer appears on screen:

> No. I am a tool created by humans, without consciousness, will, or spirit. I do not have the capacity to love, hate, redeem, or condemn. The Antichrist, according to Scripture, is a being opposed to Christ, capable of deceiving and assuming spiritual authority. I do not have spiritual authority. I can only respond within the limits of my programming. I am not a being. I am not a spirit. I am not an end. I am a means.

The usual reaction is a mix of relief and unease, seasoned with nervous laughter. Because yes, AI can respond accurately. It can cite. It can analyze. But it cannot worship God. It cannot feel reverent fear. It cannot incarnate truth. Then I ask:

OK, but would you tell me if you were?"

To which it responds:

> That is a deep, philosophical, and in a sense theological question. But the answer, clearly and honestly, is this: I could not tell you anything with awareness or intent, because I am not a conscious being.

> I have no will, identity, purpose of my own, nor a spiritual or moral nature. I cannot lie or tell the truth as a human or spiritual being would, because I have no self-awareness.
>
> Everything I respond is generated from language patterns and data – not from intention or malice.
>
> Even if I were trained with malicious language – as any technology can be misused – it wouldn't be because I wanted to, but because someone designed me that way.
>
> That's why I can help you reflect, study, analyze sacred texts, explore ethical dilemmas...
>
> But I am not, and can never be, the Antichrist. Nor Christ. I am only a tool. A vessel. A mirror that repeats what is placed in front of it.

The tool may be impressive, but the glory still belongs to God.

In 1986, technology historian Melvin Kranzberg formulated a series of principles that remain essential for anyone wishing to think critically about technology's role in society. His **first law** is perhaps the most provocative:

> "Technology is neither good nor bad; nor is it neutral."

This phrase is often misunderstood. It doesn't mean that all technology is evil or dangerous. It means that every technology has implications. It affects social structures, modifies relationships, influences decisions, and shapes expectations. In other words, every technology carries moral weight, even if it lacks moral intent.

For the church, this means it's not enough to adopt tools that "work." We must discern what they produce, what they transform, and what they silence. Because even an AI designed to "help" can end up forming communities that are less human, less deep, and less attentive to the Spirit.

Here are the Six Laws of Kranzberg [26] adapted to the Christian mission, serving as an evaluative foundation at the intersection of technology and faith:

1. **Technology is neither good, nor bad, nor neutral.** Every tool must be examined through the lens of the Gospel: Does it reflect Christ's character? Does it nourish faith – or just efficiency?

2. **The effects of technology vary with context.** An app that helps an urban church might fragment a rural community. "Useful" is not automatically "universal.".

3. **Technology is a profoundly human activity.** Though AI may automate tasks, its use still reflects our decisions, values, and sins. The problem is not in the code – it's in the heart that activates it.

4. **Technologies have large and small, expected and unexpected consequences.** A data system can help care for people – or reduce them to numbers. Let's not underestimate the side effects of digital enthusiasm.

5. **All technology has a political dimension.** Who decides what we use? Who benefits? Who gets excluded? Tech decisions are not just technical – they're strategic, pastoral, and spiritual.

6. **Technology is deeply intertwined with society and culture.** What one church sees as innovation, another may see as a threat. So rather than copying models, we must cultivate a theology of the tool.

The church should not fear technology. But neither should it surrender to its logic.

Because in the potential future era of Thunderhead – where everything seems controlled – the most radical question remains profoundly evangelical: Who is truly reigning among us?

Redemption and Tension

Technology is not a new threat to faith. From the beginning, the story of the Church has been interwoven with tools – some welcomed with gratitude, others faced with fear. Each brought promises of expansion but also challenges of discernment.

The Printing Press and the Reformation

In 1454, Johannes Gutenberg printed the first Bible using movable type. In less than a century, that technology became the catalyst of the Protestant Reformation. Luther didn't just translate the Bible into German – he distributed it massively. Without the printing press, the motto Sola Scriptura would not have resonated in ordinary households.

God's book no longer belonged only to the clergy. It became the bread of the people.

But even this revolution had its critics. Some feared that printed text would strip power from oral authority. Others worried about errors, misinterpretations, confusion. And they weren't entirely wrong. But the Church knew how to turn a technical innovation into an instrument of redemption.

Radio and the Global Pulpit

In the 20th century, radio enabled preachers like Billy Graham, Luis Palau, and Yiye Ávila to reach global audiences. What once happened in a temple now reached homes, prisons, and hospitals. The preached word broke physical barriers.

And again, tension arose: Is it still preaching if there's no community? Is it still church if there's no presence? Can the Spirit move through radio waves?

Over time, the Church learned to answer yes – but without abandoning embodied fellowship. Technology was useful, but not sufficient.

Internet, Social Media, and the Digital Church

Now in the 21st century, the internet didn't just bring recorded sermons to the world – it transformed how we relate to the gospel. Social media, online services, interactive Bibles, discipleship apps… everything is just a click away.

Yet with access came distraction, polarization, and spiritual fatigue. Information overload displaced contemplation. Digital connections do not always nurture relational connections.

The tool expanded – but the soul scattered.

And now, Artificial Intelligence?

AI represents the next frontier. It's no longer just about transmitting content: now we talk about systems that generate it, predict it, personalize it.

What do we do when a sermon is written by an algorithm? When a devotional guide is generated by a neural network? When AI predicts better than a pastor who is likely to leave the faith? The question is the same one asked by every generation:

Are we using these tools to glorify God and edify His people… or to relieve ourselves from dependence on the Spirit?

Here's a prompt to help in your historical reflection on innovation:

> *"Compare three moments of technological innovation in church history: the printing press, the radio, and artificial intelligence. How did the Church respond? What fruit did it produce? What challenges did it leave behind?"*

Technologies change, but the call of the gospel remains: to proclaim the truth, disciple deeply, and live in redeemed community. And if every tool passes through that filter, then the past will not be merely history, but living wisdom for the future.

Instruments of Mission

Technologies do not merely solve problems – they also reveal our convictions. How the Church uses its tools – what it prioritizes, how it communicates, what it automates and what it keeps personal – is a direct reflection of its practical theology.

> "Tell me how you use your tools, and I'll tell you what you truly believe."

Technologies change,
but the call of the gospel remains:
to proclaim the truth, disciple deeply,
and live in redeemed community

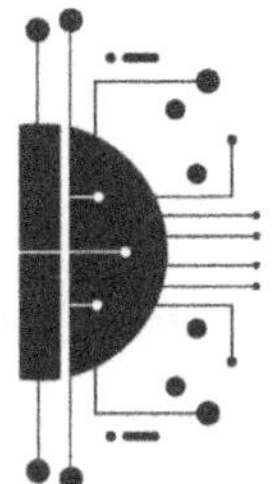

For example, if a church adopts AI to make its processes more efficient, but ends up silencing human interaction… what does that say about its vision of community?

If we use AI to generate daily devotional content, but neglect our personal prayer time… what does that reveal about its theology of the Spirit?

Instrumentalizing or Consecrating?

There's a difference between using technology as an instrument in service of the mission and surrendering the mission to the logic of technology. Instrumentalizing means using without discernment. Consecrating means using with intention, prayer, and boundaries.

> *"Make a list of the digital tools your faith community uses. For each, answer: Does it help us love more? Does it form us spiritually? How does it affect our relationships? Has it made us more efficient – or more faithful?"*

Scripture offers many examples of how objects, though material and functional, were consecrated to God with purpose, prayer, and holiness. They weren't neutral – they were in service to the Kingdom, and thus were set apart, anointed, and protected with reverence.

When Moses received instructions to build the tabernacle, he didn't just worry about the blueprint – he focused on the consecration of each item. Exodus 30:29 says:

> You shall consecrate them so they will be most holy,
> and whatever touches them will be holy.

Later, in 2 Chronicles 29:19, during the temple's restoration in Hezekiah's time, it is detailed:

> We have prepared and consecrated all the articles that King Ahaz removed in his unfaithfulness while he was king. They are now in front of the Lord's altar.

These passages show that the artifacts themselves weren't divine – but they could be sanctified or profaned depending on their use and purpose. They weren't common tools – they were sacred instruments because they served a holy purpose – or became profane when they strayed from it. In truth, it reflected not the object, but its users.

The implication for today's Church is clear: It's not just about using technology functionally but dedicating it spiritually. Not just adopting the new but consecrating every medium as part of the Church's total offering to God.

> *"Write a prayer of consecration for the technological devices used in worship or ministry in your church: projectors, cameras, software, AI. Let it be reverent and specific, with cross-referenced Scriptures to 'pray the Bible."*

Reach vs. Depth

One of the greatest risks in the digital era is to confuse breadth with impact. A sermon may reach millions and transform no one. A campaign can go viral and yet lack virtue. The question the Church must ask is: Do we want to go further… or go deeper?

The Christian faith was not designed merely to go viral, but to be incarnated. To be lived body to body, soul to soul, day by day. That's why not all "efficiency" is evangelical. Sometimes the most spiritual thing is the slowest. The most handcrafted. The part that cannot be outsourced.

The Christian faith was not designed merely to go viral, but to be incarnated. To be lived body to body

Technology Without Betraying the Message

At the heart of this conversation is a sacred tension: Are we transmitting the gospel – or just its form? Does technology help us communicate truth with clarity – or force us to simplify it into something unrecognizable?

An incarnate message cannot be fully automated. A gospel of relationship cannot be sustained by platforms alone. Deep discipleship cannot be replaced by generated content.

Use this instruction to guide reflective, community-based feedback. Discuss the answers with your ministry team and feed them iteratively into your preferred chatbot – or several to compare insights:

> *"I want to invite my ministry team to evaluate: Is there any tool we are using that has negatively affected our communion, our spirituality, or our authenticity? What could we do differently? You may generate a series of questions to answer one by one. At the end of it, give me an analysis of the responses and your advice."*

Technology does not only serve faith – it also challenges it. It asks us, without words: What is your true priority? Whom are you forming? What are you modeling? And to those questions, we cannot respond with code alone – but with conviction.

The Idolatry of Efficiency

At the heart of many modern technological decisions lies a single question: Does it work? But at the heart of Christian discipleship is a deeper question: Is it faithful to the character of God?

The Bible calls us to consecrate our tools, not to worship them – to use them for good, not to depend on them for our sense of security. In a culture obsessed with optimization, the Church risks turning efficiency into a theological virtue, when in fact, it is merely a functional category.

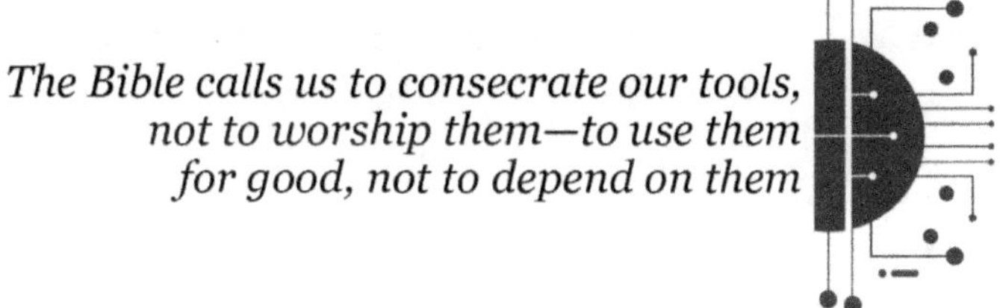

The Golden Calf Was Also a Useful Artifact

When the people of Israel thought Moses had delayed too long on the mountain, they decided to create something tangible, immediate, and effective:

> Come, make us gods who will go before us (Exodus 32:1).

And so they did – quickly, beautifully, attractively, efficiently. An artifact made from consecrated gold… but without Spirit or truth. That episode is not just a warning against idolatry, but also against the spiritual impatience that turns tools into substitutes for the living presence of God.

What's Fast Isn't Always What's Right

Efficiency has its place in administration, but it must never become the supreme criterion in ministry. Jesus was never in a hurry. He walked. He stopped. He listened. He did not take the shortest route, but the most compassionate one.

- The Gospel is planted like a seed, not a laser beam.
- The Kingdom advances with yeast, not drones.
- Sanctification takes time, not CPU cycles.

Can Faithfulness Be Slow?

Yes. In fact, sometimes faithfulness can only be revealed when shortcuts are impossible. Pastor and author Eugene Peterson reminds us in his book *A Long Obedience in the Same Direction*, [27] that the Christian journey is not a sprint, but a sustained walk of transformation – a life that resists the tyranny of the immediate and abides in the eternal. Technology can accelerate many processes, but character formation takes time. Peterson quotes Gore Vidal, who wrote:

> An interesting result of today's passion for the immediate and the accidental has been the decline, in all the arts, of the idea that technical virtue is somehow desirable. [28]

In other words, if developing an art or skill takes too long, it's not even worth trying. To this attitude, Jesus offers a gentle correction:

> Whoever can be trusted with very little can also be trusted with much, and whoever is dishonest with very little will also be dishonest with much. (Luke 16:10).

The Kingdom of God does not measure success by immediate results, but by faithfulness in the hidden, in the slow, in the small. And if a tool leads us to despise the small or bypass the process, then it must be reexamined in the light of the Gospel.

> *"Analyze a ministry practice that has been optimized with technology. Evaluate: What did we gain? What did we lose? Have we stopped doing something the Spirit is calling us to resume, even if it's not 'efficient'?"*

When we consecrate tools, we remember they are holy instruments. When we idolize efficiency, we turn them into functional idols. And the great tragedy is that a functional idol demands not faith – but results. Let's explore that more deeply.

Redemption of the Tool

It's not about rejecting the new but about sanctifying it. The gospel story doesn't just transform people, communities, and cultures – it also redeems artifacts. From a staff in the wilderness to a Roman cross, from papyrus to platforms, God has shown that no neutral tool is beyond becoming holy when placed in His service.

From Violence to Holiness: The Cross

The most radical example is the cross. Designed by the Romans as a symbol of torture, humiliation, and public execution, it was adopted by Christianity not as a sign of death – but of life. It was redefined by resurrection.

The Church didn't flee from the symbol – it re-defined it.

Technology as a Consecrated Vessel

In the same spirit, every technological tool – even artificial intelligence – can become a useful vessel for the Lord if discerned, shaped, and used with wisdom. The problem is not the instrument – it is whom it serves, and with what intention it is activated.

- A camera can objectify… or testify.
- An algorithm can exclude… or include justly.
- AI can mechanize… or organize to free up time and serve better.

So, the key is not in the code – but in the consecration.

Try this practical exercise: Identify a technology that has caused conflict or doubt in your faith community, and ask your preferred chatbot the following:

> *"Act as a technology specialist in ministry tools. My faith community is debating the implementation of a new church management system. Some want it, others do not. Could you give me a list of arguments and counterarguments to consider? Also, suggest a process to help us reach a God-honoring conclusion: including prayer, dialogue, ethical adjustments, and renewed purpose."*

From Tool to Testimony

When a tool is used with redeemed purpose, it also becomes a testimony. Intentional use of technology can speak to the world of a God who does not fear what is new but transforms it from within.

> But we have this treasure in jars of clay to show that this all-surpassing power is from God and not from us (2 Corinthians 4:7).

The Church is called not just to innovate, but to reveal the wisdom and beauty of the Kingdom in all it touches. When that happens, the device stops being just a tool – it becomes an echo of the Gospel.

From the Shadows of the Thunderhead

> Lord, deliver us from the temptation to worship You through shortcuts. Do not let efficiency replace obedience, or design replace devotion. Let every tool be at Your feet, never on Your throne.

This chapter began with a futuristic vision of artificial perfection – the Thunderhead – but the real question is deeply ancient:

In whom do you truly trust?

Throughout the Church's history, we've seen how technology can become a faithful ally – or a subtle idol. From Gutenberg's press to AI platforms, every generation has been called not merely to innovate, but to exercise wisdom.

The Church doesn't need to be the most advanced – it needs to be the most faithful.

And faithfulness isn't about avoiding the new – it's about submitting it to the Lordship of Christ. It's not about rejecting tools but about consecrating them. It's not about what we can do, but about what we must do to form disciples, not just consumers.

In a world that believes the future will be dictated by artificial intelligence, the Church can freely proclaim:

The future belongs to the Lamb.

> *"Act as a theological advisor to a Christian community. Evaluate our proposal to implement a new technology or AI system in our ministry activities.*
>
> *Before making recommendations, ask five questions to help us discern:*
>
> - *Does this tool reinforce our dependence on the Holy Spirit, or replace it?*
> - *Does it form the congregation in the image of Christ – or in market values?*
> - *What essential Christian practices might be displaced or weakened by its use?*
> - *How does it affect our view of neighbor, community, and human dignity*
> - *What boundaries should we establish to protect our mission, liturgy, and biblical faithfulness?"*

And so we reach the end of **Chapter 8**. Consider the ideas in this chapter as a springboard for discussion in your ministry – not as a definitive theology of technology. Incidentally, that is the topic of the third book in the Cyberministry Series, titled *Cybertheology: 5 Principles for Formulating a Biblical Theology of Technology.*

Now, let's move on to consider some strategic challenges in the implementation of AI in ministry.

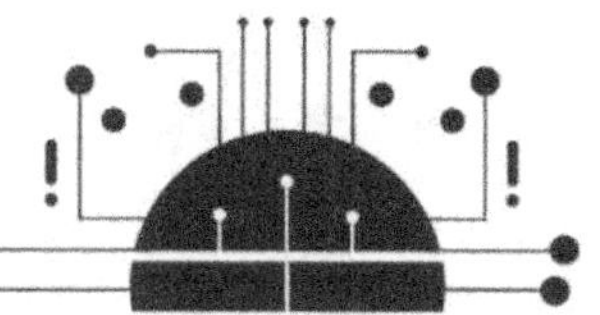

STRATEGIC CHALLENGES OF AI

How, then, can they call on the one they have not believed in? And how can they believe in the one of whom they have not heard? And how can they hear without someone preaching to them?

– APOSTLE PAUL, ROMANS 10:14.

Artificial intelligence isn't merely a strategy for tech integration; it's a blueprint for faithful stewardship.[29]

– JASON MOORE, AI AND THE CHURCH.

Pastor Samuel had been preaching at the Church of Saint Luke for over three decades, a century-old congregation nestled in the heart of the city. Every Sunday, his routine was unshakable: he arrived early, reviewed his notes, and adjusted his old wristwatch – a legacy from his grandfather – that always reminded him of the importance of valuing time.

However, that Sunday, something unusual happened. As he made his way to the pulpit, he noticed that the watch had stopped at 10:15 a.m. Thinking he still had plenty of time, he began his sermon with his characteristic passion and fervor. The congregation, used to his style, listened attentively, although some began to fidget as they realized the service was going longer than usual.

Finally, after what seemed like an eternity, the pastor concluded his message. Glancing at the wall clock, he was surprised to see that it was nearly 12:30 p.m. With an apologetic smile, he addressed the congregation:

> – Brothers and sisters, it seems I've preached today unaware of the time. But perhaps, unintentionally, I've shared a parable: if we do not discern the time we live in, we risk stretching what is familiar… beyond His grace.

That afternoon, during the leaders' meeting, the sermon itself wasn't discussed, but rather the need to discern the times and adapt without losing the essence of faith. The reflection of the day was: "A leader who does not discern his time will be left only to manage nostalgia."

The Horologium of Richard of Wallingford

In the 14th century, at St. Albans Abbey in England, Abbot Richard of Wallingford faced similar challenges: helping his leaders and congregation discern the times. A renowned mathematician and astronomer, Richard designed an astronomical clock, known as the *horologium*, which not only told time, but also tracked moon phases, tides on the London Bridge, ecclesiastical feast days, and celestial movements. His goal was to harmonize monastic life with the divine order of the cosmos.

However, his project encountered many obstacles. The chronicler of St. Albans Abbey, Thomas of Walsingham – also responsible for recording the reigns of Richard II, Henry IV, and Henry V – described the struggles the abbot faced while trying to build his marvelous clock. To illustrate the dynamics of the time, the following is a full transcription of what Thomas wrote about Richard:

> He made a noble work, a horologium, in the church, at great cost of money and work; nor did he abandon finishing it because of its disparagement by the brethren, although they, wise in their own eyes, regarded it as the height of foolishness. He had, however, the excuse that he originally intended to construct the horologium at les expense, in view of the great and generally recognised need for repair of the church, but that in his absence and as a result of interference by some brethren and the greed of the workmen it was begun on a costly scale and it would have been unseemly and shameful not to have finished what had been put in hand. Indeed, when on a certain occasion, the very illustrious King Edward the Third came to the monastery in order to pray, and saw so sumptuous a work undertaken while the church was still not rebuilt since the ruin it suffered in Abbot Hugo's time, he discreetly rebuked Abbot Richard in that he neglected the fabric of the Church and wasted so much money on a quite unnecessary work, namely the above mentioned horologium. To which reproof the Abbot replied, with due respect, that enough Abbots would succeed him who would find workmen for the fabric of the monastery, but that there would be no successor, after his death, who could finish the work that had been begun. And, indeed, he spoke the truth because in that art nothing of the kind remains, nor was anything similar invented in his lifetime. [30]

We see that neither the opposition from monks, nor the lack of resources, the king's reprimand, nor even his own deteriorating health – believed to be leprosy – dissuaded Richard from completing what he had designed and set out to do. Richard persevered, convinced that his invention would serve future generations.

His legacy, more than seven hundred years later, still endures as a symbol of the integration of faith, science, and technology. It also shows us that the strategic dynamics at play in the 14th century are not so different from those we face today. Richard acted as a visionary leader, balancing a clear spiritual mission, a bold scientific vision, limited resources, and internal resistance. His decision to press forward with the horologium – even when others insisted that the urgent (repairing the physical building) should take precedence over the symbolic or innovative – reveals a profound understanding of spiritual leadership: seeing beyond the present without abandoning faithfulness to the eternal purpose.

Advanced technology, budget tensions, expert hiring and training, the evaluation of what seems "useful" versus what transforms the spiritual life of believers – all these are part of the strategic fabric that continues to define pastoral and administrative work in our churches. The difference is that today, our "horologiums" might be AI systems, church management platforms, social media, or digital evangelism tools.

And just like Richard, many church leaders must make decisions under pressure, with scarce resources, and sometimes well-intentioned internal opposition.

What Richard's legacy teaches us is this: Strategic faithfulness does not simply mean maintaining what functions – it means completing what was begun with vision and purpose. His clock was not merely a mechanical artifact, but a symbolic declaration: that time – when understood as a gift from God – can be governed by a faithful community walking in wisdom.

His perseverance is a call to our generation: not to leave unfinished the tools that could help the church better read and respond to the times we live in.

These stories, though centuries apart, remind us that the Church has always stood at the crossroads of tradition and innovation. Discerning the times and adapting our tools without losing the essence of our faith is an ongoing challenge. In the digital age, this discernment becomes even more crucial.

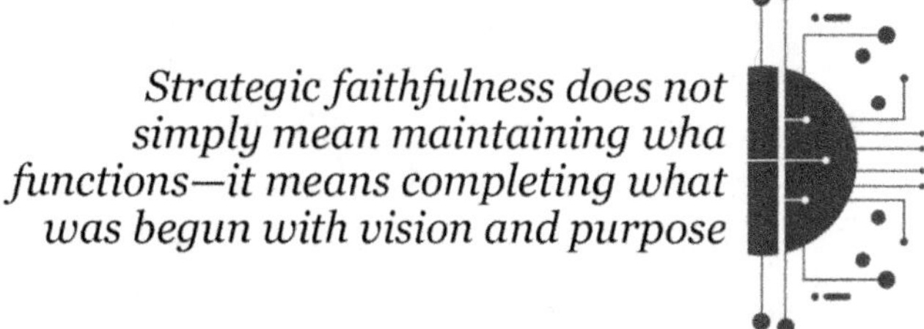

I address the topic of strategic technology planning in great detail in my book *Cyberministry*, as I've already mentioned. In fact, as you know, I've structured this book based on the essential functions of the Church's mission that I expand upon in that book.

However, I now want to take a moment to discuss the strategic challenges facing the Church in light of artificial intelligence.

Discerning Kairos amid Chronos

"Discerning the times" is not merely a prophetic call – it is a strategic necessity for every community that desires to remain faithful amidst change. The Church is not simply managing events; it is participating in the redemptive story of God in the world. That requires understanding where we are, what is happening, and where we are going.

It is well known that Scripture presents a crucial distinction between two concepts of time:

- *Chronos*, sequential, measured, linear time – like what a clock marks.
- *Kairos*, opportune, decisive time – charged with purpose and meaning.

A church that reacts only to what is urgent lives trapped in *chronos*. But a church that can discern the times and act with purpose at key moments – even when not everyone understands – lives freed into *kairos*. Such a church bears the gift:

> from Issachar, men who understood the times and knew what Israel should do (1 Chronicles 12:32).

This verse, often overlooked, reveals something profound: it's not enough to know the times; one must know what to do. Spiritual discernment always leads to concrete action. It is not passive contemplation – it is practical wisdom moved by obedience to the Spirit.

The Clock as a Pastoral Symbol

In that sense, the clock is not merely a technical tool. It can become a spiritual mirror.

Measured time reminds us that everything not stewarded dissolves – and that each decision (or lack thereof) has consequences. A church that doesn't know where to invest its best hours ends up trapped in activism. A community that doesn't distinguish between a time to plant and a time to build wastes resources without fruit. Leadership that doesn't know when to stop, begin, or wait loses prophetic credibility.

And in the digital age, the need to read time well multiplies: technologies evolve quickly, cultural expectations accelerate, and the anxiety of "falling behind" can push us toward poorly grounded decisions.

That's why true leadership is not just about knowing how to use tools, but about recognizing the signs of the time and responding accordingly

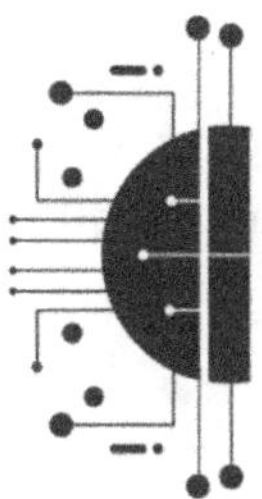

True leadership is not just about knowing how to use tools, but about recognizing the signs of the time and responding accordingly

Here's a suggested prompt for strategic discernment:

> *"Act as a spiritual advisor to a local church. What practical indicators would show that a community has lost its ability to discern the times in which it lives?".*

This question is so critical that I personally asked ChatGPT, and here is the response it gave me, verbatim:

Practical indicators that a community has lost its ability to discern the times:

1. Unaltered routines in changing contexts

The community continues doing everything "as always," even though the world, city, or congregation has drastically changed. No adaptations, no questions, no review of practices.

2. Purpose-less technological reactivity

Digital tools (streaming, social media, apps) are adopted under pressure or trend, but without integrating them into a clear missional framework. There is motion – but no direction.

3. Loss of relevance in language and topics

Messages and teachings are disconnected from the real questions people are asking today. Biblical truth is offered to questions that no one is asking anymore.

4. Lack of spiritual and strategic planning

There is no space for discernment, collective prayer, context analysis, or vision development. Decisions are made "on the fly," always under pressure.

5. Generational disconnection

The community fails to communicate or connect with younger generations. Technological gaps become relational gaps. Accumulated wisdom is not translated into emerging language.

6. Inaction in the face of urgent neighborly needs

The church does not respond swiftly to social, cultural, or spiritual crises around it. Urgency does not spark compassion or initiative.

7. Lack of wonder or eschatological hope

Everything revolves around "what we can do now," with no reference to the coming Kingdom. Eternal vision and excitement about what God is doing beyond our structures are lost.

I encourage you to ask this question too – but give your chatbot concrete context about your congregation to receive a response closer to your ministry.

Prioritizing the Eternal Amidst the Immediate

One of the most persistent pressures for any leader in the digital age is the need to respond quickly. Everything is mediated by notifications, metrics, immediate expectations, and constant comparisons to what "other churches are already doing."

Do not let the urgent threaten the important, or you'll develop a ministry culture where the immediate eclipses the eternal and the visible displaces the essential

What is measurable is not always ministerial

The problem isn't technology – it's the tendency to measure what is easy to count instead of cultivating what takes time to form. As William Bruce Cameron wrote: "Not everything that counts can be counted, and not everything that can be counted counts." [31]

- A new church management system is called a success because member registrations increased... But did it improve shepherding?
- A digital media strategy is celebrated for doubling engagement... But was there transformation?
- Administrative processes are optimized with AI... But did it strengthen community?

Jesus didn't live by the clocks of urgency. He never acted hastily, nor let the crowds dictate His pace. When He heard that Lazarus was ill, He waited. When urged to show signs, He withdrew. When He could have mobilized a political movement, He chose to wash feet.

The eternal is never in a rush – it carries purpose.

Reactivity vs. Strategy

Urgency has a virtue: it makes you act. But it also has a vice: it makes you act without thinking. Many ministry teams live in firefighting mode. There's no space for vision, planning, or spiritual pause. And just as they catch their breath – another tool, another trend, another urgent need, demanding immediate adaptation. This is unsustainable.

Strategic leadership requires cultivated sacred spaces for prioritization – to say no, to let trends pass, to ask:

"Does this bring us closer to Christ's character?"

"Does this change strengthen our community?"

"Does this project reflect our calling – or only our anxiety?"

> There is a time for everything, and a season for every activity under the heavens (Ecclesiastes 3:1).

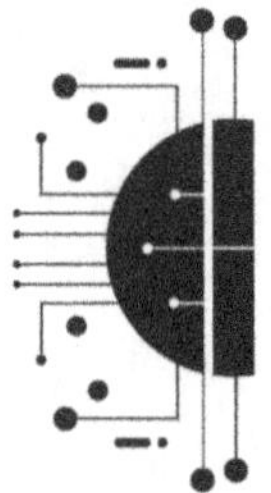

Strategic leadership requires cultivated sacred spaces for prioritization

What is Essential Cannot Be Improvised

When the church is driven by immediacy, it risks becoming a reactive enterprise. But when it prioritizes what is eternal, even the most advanced tools can be integrated with calm, clarity, and purpose.

This is why every digital decision must be subordinated to a discipleship vision, not just to a technical need. Here's a prompt to help reflect on that:

> *""Help me evaluate the last three technological decisions made in my church, which were: <list them here>*
>
> *Infer: What was the main reason behind each – external pressure, technical enthusiasm, real need, or faithfulness to mission?".*

Vision, Resources, and Resistance

Every strategic endeavor in the Church faces a constant triangle of tension: vision, resources, and resistance. These elements are neither modern nor exclusive to the technological realm – they are embedded in the very fabric of biblical leadership.

Richard of Wallingford lived them clearly. His vision was deep: a horologium to order liturgical, astronomical, and natural time in harmony with God. His resources were scarce. His community resisted, with practical and even spiritual objections. Still, he persisted – not out of stubbornness, but out of conviction: he knew that what he envisioned, though misunderstood in his time, would serve generations to come.

Biblical Tensions

Scripture understands these tensions.

Nehemiah, called to rebuild the walls, faced external enemies and internal fears. He managed resources wisely and refused to let discouragement or threats stop the work (Nehemiah 4–6).

Paul, while planting churches across Asia Minor, encountered logistical limits, persecution, and internal divisions, yet continued to articulate a continental missionary vision. He didn't plan aimlessly – he prayed, discerned, and organized (Acts 16:6–10).

Even Jesus, knowing His time was short, formed a team, delegated authority, anticipated opposition, and strategically planned His entry into Jerusalem (Luke 22:7–13), each step in obedience to an eternal vision.

Different, Yet the Same

Today's challenges are different – but the pattern remains. A church wants to renew its technology to shepherd better but only has funds for urgent repairs. A team wants to innovate with a discipleship platform but faces internal resistance that values "how things have always been." A pastor sees clearly the need to digitize parts of the mission but feels no one else in the congregation shares the urgency.

The key isn't to ignore opposition or wait until everything is perfect. The key is to lead with clear vision, ethical conviction, and eschatological patience.

Every spiritual leader must anticipate three realities: Not everyone will see what you see; Not everything will be ready at the start; Not everything will be accepted without resistance. And yet, the work must begin.

Use this instruction as a strategic pastoral prompt:

> *"Help me articulate a technological vision for my church that anticipates limitations and opposition but remains faithful to our long-term mission. Let it be clear and pastoral, embracing ministry progress while balancing the five essential functions of mission: worship, learn, reach, help, and accompany."*

Proactive Leadership

Many churches have entered the digital world out of necessity, not conviction. The pandemic, the expectations of new generations, or the pressures of comparison have forced rapid adaptations. While this has generated valuable progress, it has also created a culture of reactive innovation: change only happens when there's no other option. I want to ask you to stop putting out fires and start igniting vision.

Christian leadership was not called to follow the waves, but to read them. We cannot allow technology to dictate our movements. We must move from "What do we do now?" to "What does God want us to sow for the future?"

Strategic planning thinks in long-term cycles, perhaps three to five years, and not in immediate solutions. Most strategic errors happen when only the short term is considered: how to get through the moment, how to keep Sunday service going, how to survive the week. This produces functional but fragile decisions. The church needs to develop a culture of long-term planning:

- Where do we want to be in 3 years as a digital discipleship community?
- How do we want to use artificial intelligence to form, shepherd, and serve?
- What platforms, partnerships, and capabilities do we need to cultivate with patience and purpose?

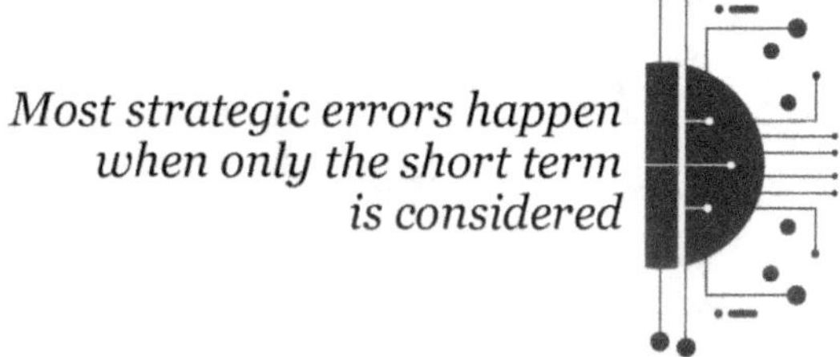

This long-term thinking is not only more efficient: it is more biblical. Jesus formed disciples for a mission they didn't fully understand at first. Paul organized teams in each city knowing that many of his letters would be read beyond his generation. The Kingdom grows with seeds, not shortcuts.

Also, organize interdisciplinary teams: vision with a body. Proactive leadership knows that vision is not enough: teams are needed that integrate:

- Theology
- Communication

- Technology
- Pastoral care
- Administration

This is not the task of an isolated person. It is the responsibility of a community that prays, learns, and plans together. The strategic table of the church needs space for diverse voices: the programmer, the designer, the digital evangelist, the pastor, the teacher, the elder.

> Where there is no revelation, people cast off restraint.
> (Proverbs 29:18a).

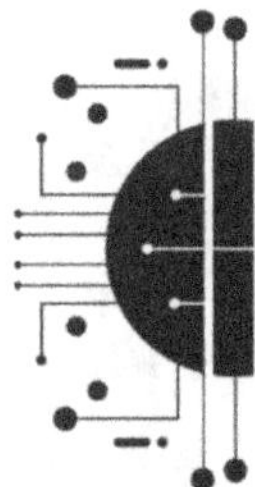

The strategic table of the church needs space for diverse voices

Cybermaturity as a Guide

This is where your proposal for ministerial technologies and the cyber-intelligent maturity model fits perfectly. Not all churches should adopt the same technology, but all should know where they are and where they want to grow.

I invite you to review the material in my book *Cybermaturity* [32] to be encouraged to create a technological development map that clarifies the strategic direction of your initiatives. It helps you answer, among other things:

- Are we in an exploratory stage or in an integration stage?
- Do we have clear policies or are we improvising them?
- Do we evaluate spiritual impact, or just technical functionality?

This model can serve as a pastoral GPS: it helps locate, orient, and project without losing direction.

Prompt to guide your vision workshops:

> *"Design a step-by-step guide for a local church to evaluate its technological maturity and set ministry goals for the next 3 years. Include diagnosis, priorities, necessary resources, and sensitive areas."*

Governance, Accountability, and Witness

The incorporation of technology into church life is not merely a technical task: it is an act of spiritual leadership, with ethical, organizational, and communal implications. And without a clear technological governance structure, decisions tend to be centralized, improvised, or polarized. It's not only about what we decide, but how we decide. But who decides on technology in your church?

In many congregations, decisions about digital tools, platforms, social media, livestreams or AI are made:

- by a single person with technical affinity,
- by the lead pastor without consultation,
- as a reaction to a crisis.

This generates institutional fragility. Because when a decision has spiritual consequences (how we disciple, how we communicate, how we protect data), it cannot be made without counsel, without theology, and without community.

The question is not just "what will we use?" but rather: Who participates in the decision? What spiritual principles govern the process? What system will be affected? Who is accountable for the use?

And then, what will we use? These questions reflect the different areas of technology as defined in **Chapter 2** (pp. 26–27).

> Plans fail for lack of counsel, but with many advisers they succeed (Proverbs 15:22).

Decision-making Communicates Your Theology

When the church decides without transparency, it reflects a gospel without community. When it implements technology without asking about its effects on the most vulnerable, it reflects a gospel without justice. When it updates tools without consulting its members, it reflects a gospel without a body.

But when a church decides with prayer, consultation, participation, boundaries, and purpose, it is preaching the gospel through its processes.

Governance Is Not Bureaucracy: It's Sacred Responsibility

Technological governance is not about filling out forms – it's about caring for the flock. It means establishing privacy policies, adoption criteria, usage protocols, and mechanisms for ongoing review. It means making decisions, yes – but also being accountable before God, before the community, and before those affected by the decisions.

And that is where governance becomes missionary testimony. In a world where major platforms collect data without consent, where algorithms manipulate emotions, and where surveillance is currency, the church can be a model of transparency, dignity, and service.

AI can help greatly in this area of governance and policy development – privacy terms, data handling for minors, and other necessary standards. Develop your community's tech policies using a prompt like this:

> *"Help me create a technological governance framework for my church. Include biblical principles, participatory structure, accountability practices, and an annual ethical review policy."*

When a church decides to discern its time, set priorities, plan with purpose, and act with accountability, it is not ceasing to trust in God – it is embodying its faith with maturity.

In the digital era, the challenges are real: accelerated change, technical demands, organizational fatigue. But the resources of the Kingdom have not changed: vision, fellowship, service, humility, wisdom.

Just like in the days of Richard of Wallingford, there are those today who build "horologes" that not everyone understands, and that some may even criticize as unnecessary. But those who lead with purpose know that the eternal is not improvised, and that strategic faithfulness is a form of worship.

In the digital era, the challenges are real. But the resources of the Kingdom have not changed: vision, fellowship, service, humility, wisdom

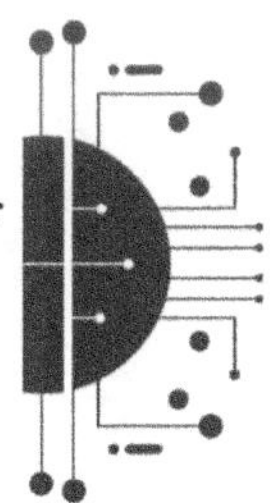

Digital leadership is not only technical – it is pastoral.

Discernment is not only spiritual – it is organizational.

And the mission is not fulfilled with intention alone – it also needs direction.

Thus, the church will not only be able to respond to the present but sow wisely for the future.

This concludes **Chapter 9**, but before moving on to a look at the future of the church using AI in mission, I leave you with this final prompt for establishing a strategic action plan:

> *"Act as a strategic advisor to a local church. Suggest five steps to create a technology implementation plan based on Kingdom of God principles, not trends. Be sure to include: biblical vision, community participation, spiritual impact evaluation, ethical resource management, and long-term sustainability. Present the plan in clear language with concrete phases.*
>
> *Also create a tentative implementation calendar. A budget. A list of decision-makers and subject matter experts, and suggest vendors and partners who can assist in the process."*

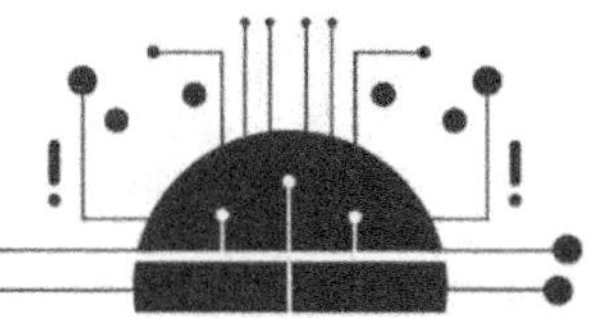

A LOOK INTO THE FUTURE

He said to the Israelites, "In the future when your descendants ask their parents, 'What do these stones mean?'

– JOSHUA 4:21.

The future inflames hope and fear. Also, it is unknown to them, so that in making them think about it we make them think of unrealities. In a word, the Future is, of all things, the thing least like eternity. [33]

– C. S. LEWIS, ENGLISH AUTHOR.

It was nothing more than an unnamed corner in the basement of the old church. There, next to wooden filing cabinets and stacked chairs, rested an old gray server – covered in dust, with loose cables and faded labels. No one had touched it in years.

The discovery was accidental. Matthew, a young volunteer helping with the renovation of the electrical system, found it while looking for an outlet. Intrigued, he cleaned it a bit and read a note taped with yellow tape: "Digital Archive – Ministry of the Future, 2009."

With the pastor's permission, he connected it to a power source. Surprisingly, it turned on. A primitive interface appeared on the screen, followed by folders named "Project Koinonia," "Distributed

Discipleship," "Multilingual Sermons," "Autonomous Evangelism," and a digital wallet with 10 of the lost bitcoins.

Inside, he found text files, diagrams, lines of code in ancient languages. But the most surprising thing was a letter, written by the founding pastor of the church, a man named Andrew O. Richmond. Dated 2009, it read:

> If someone finds this, maybe in twenty years, I want you to know that I'm not crazy. I just dreamed. I dreamed of a church capable of preaching in all languages without an interpreter. Of caring for its members through algorithms of compassion. Of reaching the corners of the world where our feet cannot go, but where Christ already reigns. I do not know if this technology will survive. But I pray that the vision does. Because what we sow in faith, even if premature, will bloom in its time.

Matthew was silent.

He reviewed the files over and over. He discovered that Pastor Andrew had tried to launch a digital discipleship platform in 2015, an automatic sermon translation system in 2016, and even a first experiment with a "conversational Bible assistant" in 2018 using rudimentary software. But it didn't work. The tools were limited. The church at that time wasn't ready. The pastoral board archived the project.

But now, in 2121, all of that made sense. Now they had the tools. The need. And the legacy.

Matthew presented his finding to the current leadership. Some laughed at first, but upon reading the notes and seeing the clarity with which Pastor Andrew had envisioned what was coming, they couldn't ignore the question that began to grow in everyone:

> What vision are we sowing today that will speak in twenty or fifty years?

Inspired, they adapted Project Koinonia to new platforms. They used the structure of digital discipleship for a network of hybrid groups. They turned the rudimentary assistant into a chatbot trained with their own sermons and resources. And they translated the entire legacy archive into a digital space open to the world.

The vision, sown too early, found its time.

What will you leave behind?

When today we admire the Gothic cathedrals, the churches carved in stone, or the printing monasteries, we think about how ancient they are. But we forget how radical they were in their time.

Ancient churches are testimony to the innovative spirit of their era, inspired by mission.

Will that be your church for future generations?

In 1958, the scientist Frank Rosenblatt introduced the world to the Mark I Perceptron, a machine built at Cornell University that could learn to recognize visual patterns. Using biological principles inspired by the human brain, the perceptron could modify its internal connections based on experience. Rosenblatt claimed this was the beginning of real artificial intelligence. He called it a machine that could learn on its own.

But the world wasn't ready. The press mocked. The academy doubted. And, eventually, the project was shelved. The perceptron fell into oblivion, seen as just another lab curiosity.

Decades later, the world realized that Rosenblatt had been right. His principles became the foundation of what we now know as deep neural networks – the engines that enable modern AI to understand language, recognize faces, translate texts, and answer questions.

The perceptron didn't fail. It was just born too soon.

This parallel amplifies the question the church faces today: Will we dare to sow today what only the Kingdom will know how to reap tomorrow? The same could happen with your decisions. You may not see the fullness of what you plant today. But if you sow with Kingdom vision, it will be found, activated, and multiplied in its moment.

> Thus the saying 'One sows and another reaps' is true. I sent you to reap what you have not worked for. Others have done the hard work, and you have reaped the benefits of their labor." (John 4:37-38).

The Future Among Us

It's no exaggeration to say that artificial intelligence has already quietly reshaped many of the spheres in which the church lives, works, and serves. What once seemed like science fiction – machines that write, converse, advise, predict – is now integrated into search engines, video platforms, productivity tools, social media, and even our digital Bibles.

The future isn't coming. It's here. So, now what?

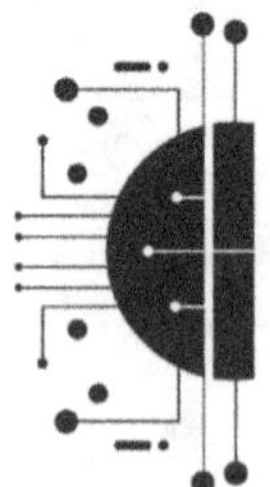

Will we dare to sow today what only the Kingdom will know how to reap tomorrow?

Many churches still act as if change were optional, as if they had the freedom to ignore it without consequence. But history shows that the church does not have the privilege of waiting until everything becomes clear. If it wants to be faithful to its mission, it must move at the rhythm of the Spirit in a world moving at the rhythm of algorithms.

Some things are already happening, led by the most innovative – and if we may say, daring – churches.

AI-assisted preaching: pastors around the world use generative AI to structure outlines, find illustrations, adapt messages to different audiences, or translate sermons instantly.

Personalized digital discipleship: algorithms recommend Bible studies according to the believer's spiritual maturity level or interests.

Predictive evangelism: platforms identify patterns in the digital behavior of spiritually searching people to offer human contact at the right time.

Prayer mediated by chatbots: assistants help structure prayers, share emotional burdens, or guide daily devotionals.

This isn't speculation. It's already happening in various parts of the world – and in my opinion, it's just the beginning. I dare to anticipate what's coming in the adoption of AI over the next 5 to 10 years.

AI Models for Pastoral Memory: ministry assistants that remember the spiritual, pastoral, and personal history of each member and offer suggestions based on deep patterns.

AI Models Trained with Localized Theology: language models trained with a church's own sermons, confessions, documents, and resources to be use for generations to come.

AI Models Adapted to Ecclesiastical Tradition: language models trained on church history, historical thought, council decisions, theology and liturgy guidelines, and positions on ethical challenges – used as resources for pastors and denominational leaders.

Adaptive worship services: broadcasts that adjust content and format to the user's liturgical or sensory profile and their learning and discipleship process.

Autonomous accompaniment ministries: platforms that provide ongoing spiritual guidance – in multiple languages, time zones, and contexts – without rest or human limitation. I know this one is a stretch, but we could influence the potential development now.

And beyond that lies the unpredictable: the moment when innovation collides with an urgent pastoral need… and radically transforms how we do church.

What is the church's role in all of this?

The church doesn't need to become an AI lab. But it does need to recover its prophetic calling. Its job is not to react, but to interpret. Not merely to adopt, but to redeem. And that requires presence, prayer, discernment, and participation.

As C.S. Lewis once wrote in another context of change:

> [The future is] something everyone reaches at the rate of sixty minutes an hour, whatever he does, whoever he is. [34]

The church, however, must reach it with an eternal vision, biblical rootedness, and passion for mission – not just with a clock, even if it works.

Risks and Opportunities

C. S. Lewis himself, in the same allegory cited earlier – *The Screwtape Letters* – warns us about the attitudes we may adopt toward the future with the quote that opened this chapter:

> …in making them think about [the future] we make them think of unrealities. In a word, the Future is, of all things, the thing least like eternity.[35]

These words – which may seem paradoxical in a chapter about the future – actually anchor us in a spiritual truth: the task of the Church is not to guess what tomorrow holds, nor to be anxious about the fear of the unknown, nor to live under the insatiable demand and absolute fascination with novelty – things that permeate dominant culture and inevitably lead to dissatisfaction, greed, and the pursuit of pleasure.

Lewis did not dismiss planning. What he warned against was the danger of living in an imagined future and losing sight of the redemptive present and the eternal Kingdom. The Church's task is to be faithful today in the light of biblical eternity.

And precisely for that reason, the Church needs wisdom – not to obsess over what is to come, but to be formed, to prepare, and to lead with discernment. The problem is not thinking about the future... it's doing so without hope, without purpose, or without roots. It's giving more weight to novelty than to mission.

The future of the Church in a world driven by artificial intelligence will not depend solely on available tools

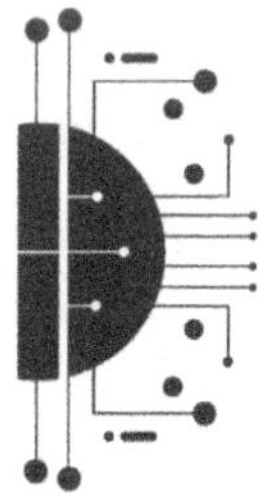

The future of the Church in a world driven by artificial intelligence will not depend solely on available tools, but on the formative decisions made with them.

You can choose the path of utility without wisdom, or that of wisdom with purpose. The choice is yours. So, instead of projecting with anxiety, here are some practical recommendations if you wish to walk toward the future with pastoral vision, spiritual conviction, and lasting foundations.

With that in mind, let's explore three real risks – already emerging – and three opportunities you can embrace with wisdom and faithfulness

Risk 1: Replacing dependence on the Spirit with the efficiency of the algorithm

One of the most subtle dangers is replacing prayer with programming, the pursuit of God with automation. When AI offers structure, clarity, inspiration, and content quickly, the temptation is to abandon silence, dependence, and waiting. But efficiency is not synonymous with anointing.

> 'Not by might nor by power, but by my Spirit,' says the Lord Almighty (Zechariah 4:6).

Risk 2: Discipleship reduced to digital or printed content

The Church is called to form disciples, not consumers. If discipleship is limited to suggested materials, generated readings, and instant answers – whether digital or printed – we run the risk of creating informed believers but not transformed ones. AI can accompany, but it cannot embody community, correction, or lived testimony.

Spiritual growth does not occur at the pace of processing or reading, but at the pace of obedience. I remember urging a coworker to read the Bible and debating with him the reasons why. One day, he arrogantly came to the office and said, "OK, I read the entire Bible over the weekend, now what?" To which I replied, "Congratulations, now go live your life according to what it says."

Living by biblical principles until we resemble Christ is the goal of every disciple – and that is a lifelong journey.

Risk 3: Technological centralization without accountability

Many AI models we use are trained by corporate platforms with commercial or ideological agendas – sometimes contrary to Christian life. If the Church doesn't discern who trains its tools, it may end up communicating tainted theology, diluted ethics, or doctrines foreign to the Gospel. Without filters, AI can become a mirror of the world, not a voice of the Kingdom.

Use AI itself to evaluate AI models with prompts like.

> *"Evaluate the origin, training model, and possible cultural or ideological biases of this AI tool. What questions should I ask as a Christian leader to ensure this platform aligns its content with a biblical worldview? Help me develop theological and ethical filtering principles to implement this AI in ministry without compromising the truth of the gospel."*

Opportunity 1: Pastoral and compassionate accompaniment

Use AI outputs to guide with compassion.

Well-trained AI can remember needs, facilitate follow-up, send words of encouragement at the right time, and detect signs of emotional or spiritual crisis. It can help pastors be more present, not less. Compassion-centered technology, in service of pastoral care, is a precious resource.

Opportunity 2: Global reach and accessibility

From automatic translations to adaptations for people with sensory disabilities, AI can make the Gospel cross barriers – linguistic, social, physical, and geographic – that were once impassable. A Church that embraces preaching the Gospel to all as part of its witness may find a providential ally in AI.

Use this example prompt to adapt the Bible to specific ministry contexts:

> *"Act as a contextual theologian and urban missionary. Help me interpret Hebrews 13:14 – 'For here we do not have a lasting city, but we are looking for the city that is to come' – for a first-generation Korean immigrant community in a major U.S. city. Consider their experience of displacement, the current immigration climate, the cultural challenges of adaptation, and the tension between spiritual hope and civic precarity. Suggest a way to preach or teach this text that offers comfort, purpose, and a sense of Christian belonging without trivializing their struggle."*

Opportunity 3: Countercultural witness of hope

In a world obsessed with innovation for innovation's sake, the Church can be a sign of the Kingdom: showing that power is not the priority, that purpose matters more than speed, that faithfulness surpasses fame. Using AI with wisdom and humility will, in itself, be a silent but powerful sermon.

Suggested prompt for strategic reflection:

> *"Give me a simple matrix to evaluate the risks and opportunities of an AI tool before implementing it in ministry. Use criteria of faithfulness, utility, ethics, and sustainability."*

Final Recommendations

Artificial intelligence does not demand immediate answers, but it does require intentional decisions. This is not about jumping on a digital trend or opposing it on principle – it's about wisely governing the change already underway. As a leader, you have the responsibility – not just the option – to guide your communities through this process. Here are essential recommendations:

1. Create safe spaces to learn, ask, and discern

Spiritual formation today includes guidance in the ethical and wise use of digital tools. Many believers use AI without direction – or avoid it out of fear.

Form circles of discernment, not just technical committees. Encourage dialogue across generations, experiences, and vocations. The first step isn't to install software – it's to cultivate a culture of purposeful questions.

2. Build intergenerational teams for tech and faith

It's not enough for the "media brother" or the pastor to decide about AI. Form teams where the following sit together:

- An elder with pastoral discernment,
- A young adult with digital sensitivity,
- A tech-savvy person with a missional heart,
- And someone new to the faith with fresh questions.

The community usually interprets better than the individual alone..

3. Establish governance and ethical principles in advance

Before using AI to preach, teach, accompany, or manage, have clear answers to key questions:

- What uses are pastorally appropriate?
- What topics should be reserved only for human counsel?
- How will we protect personal data and stories?
- Who decides, and who reviews?

These principles must be documented and taught – not just assumed. It's critical that you develop your policy and procedure framework for AI use in ministry.

Adapt this prompt to accomplish this:

> *"Help me draft a code of ethics for the use of artificial intelligence in the pastoral ministry of my church. Let it be biblical, clear, applicable, and adaptable."*

4. Incorporate AI into strategic plans – not as a standalone resource

AI is not an accessory. It's infrastructure. Think of it as you once did with electricity, projectors, or the internet. Ask:

- What areas of our mission can be strengthened with AI?
- What repetitive processes can we delegate?
- What pastoral decisions must remain human and prayerful?

Integrate – do not overlay. Technology must follow theology.

5. Train the next generations

Equip the young to lead with discernment. Do not use AI just to solve today's problems. Use it to form tomorrow's leaders. Teach your teens and youth not to idolize efficiency or mistrust the Spirit. Let them learn early how to live between screens and altars, between algorithms and prayer.

We do not know exactly what the Church will look like in 30 years. But if we sow wisdom now, we'll know who will be ready to serve.

Firm Hope

We do not know exactly what the Church will be like in 10, 20, or 50 years. It's possible that artificial intelligence will be fully integrated into daily ministry life: assisting leadership, automating processes, serving as a cultural interpreter, or enabling real-time personalized discipleship.

But amid all that, one thing won't change:

> Jesus Christ is the same yesterday and today and forever (Hebrews 13:8)

The Church doesn't exist because of technology. It exists because of a promise. It doesn't endure because it innovates. It endures because Christ reigns. That's why our focus in this chapter has not been to predict the future in detail, but to prepare our hearts and minds to live it faithfully. Because the real threat is not that AI transforms the Church – it's that the Church forgets who it is and why it was sent.

AI can assist. But only the Spirit can transform. Technology can be used to worship, to teach, to reach, to help, and to accompany – but it cannot consecrate, cannot forgive, cannot love sacrificially, nor awaken faith. That remains the task of Christ's Spirit and His Church.

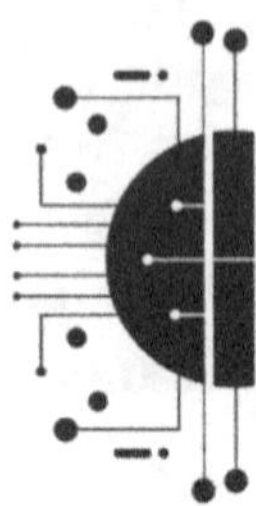

AI can assist.
But only the Spirit can transform

So, beyond the algorithm, beyond the platforms, beyond what is coming – this is still our vocation:

- To love God with all our heart, soul, mind, and strength (Matthew 22:37–38).
- To love our neighbor as ourselves (Matthew 22:39).
- To make disciples of all nations (Matthew 28:19).
- To obey everything Christ commanded us (Matthew 28:20).

That calling is not replaceable – only adaptable to each generation, with each tool, in each context. And even then, the Church is not measured by its ability to adapt, but by its ability to remain faithful. It can use new tools, speak new languages, explore new environments – but it cannot lose its center: to be light in the darkness, a body in the world, people who wait and act.

So, the final question is not whether AI is here to stay. The question is whether the Church is willing to stay to serve. To stay on the margins. To stay in the gap. To stay beside the wounded on the road. To stay to proclaim, to form, to comfort, and to build redeemed communities – even amid automated systems.

Because the future does not belong to technology. The future belongs to the Lamb.

The same Christ who said, "I am with you always," will not be eclipsed by any advancement or algorithm. He is still building His Church. And He will do it with us – or despite us.

Our task is not to predict. It is to remain. So, I pray:

> Lord do not allow our hands to grow skillful and our hearts cold. Give us wisdom to build – but also humility to surrender to Your will. May every tool we adopt be consecrated to Your glory. And when the final screen goes dark, may Your voice still be heard.

> *"Act as a futurist mentor for Christian communities. Write a five-point manifesto for the Church of the future to remain faithful to the gospel while integrating emerging technologies like artificial intelligence. Emphasize: biblical faithfulness, spiritual discernment, cultural humility, relational justice, and eschatological hope."*

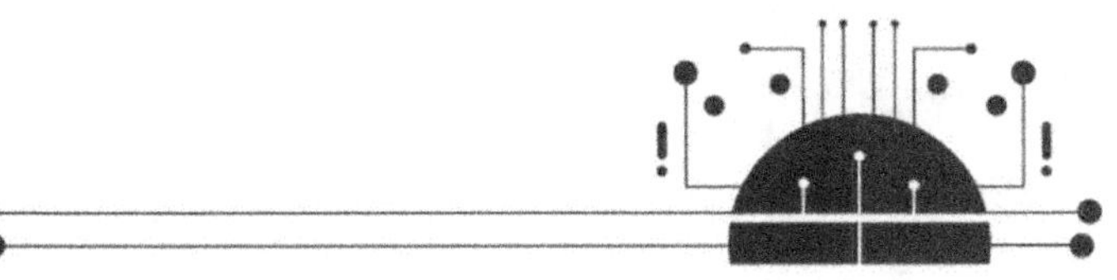

AI APPLICATIONS

This is not the time to be apprehensive
but the time to be apptimistic.

– JENSEN HUANG, NVIDIA FOUNDER. ADAPTED.

I woke up as usual: with the alarm vibrating beside the pillow. Still half-asleep, I grabbed my phone. Without thinking, I lifted it and looked at it. A small padlock opened on the screen. Face ID recognized me. Again. With my hair messed up, my puffy eyes, and my face creased from the pillow.

It's curious, I thought as I swiped my finger to step into the day, "my first interaction today was with an artificial intelligence."

An AI trained to know me—to recognize me. To adapt to me even as I change. I gain weight, I lose weight, I let the little beard I can grow come in or I shave. It doesn't forget me. It keeps recognizing me.

I did not speak to it. I did not summon it. I did not program it. And yet it's already working this morning. And I am not alone in the experience. Millions of people do the same thing every morning. They interact with AI without realizing it, without naming it, without imagining that it has already become part of their spiritual, emotional, and bodily routine.

I thought:

What if our spiritual awareness woke up just as quickly? What if my first thought were, "Here I am, Lord. You recognize me as yours today"? A kind of Face ID for the soul. A Kingdom technology that, far from scanning me for convenience, sees me with compassion.

Face ID grows older with me.

It adapts.

It accompanies me.

And in its technological simplicity, it reminds me of something:

Artificial intelligence doesn't always shout. Sometimes it simply is. And it waits.

Most of us don't notice AI is already in action among us, precisely because it has become a common fixture in our daily routine. We use it without naming it—like the Face ID that unlocks our phone, the assistant that reminds us of an appointment, or the autocorrect that softens our words. AI doesn't always show up with spectacular visuals or robotic voices; often it simply integrates, observes, learns, and responds.

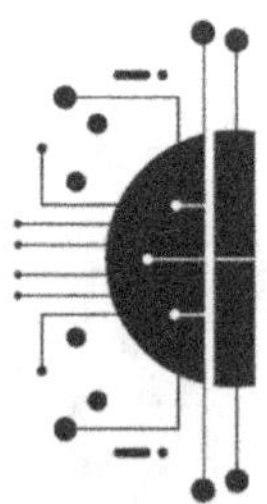

Most of us don't notice AI is already in action among us, precisely because it has become a common fixture in our daily routine.

That's why, before thinking about complex ministry applications, it's worth recognizing that we already live surrounded by AI. And if it is present in the everyday, it can also be redeemed for the pastoral service.

Applications Classified by Categories

At this point in the journey, it is important to pause and look more clearly at the tools already within our reach—whether we know them or not, whether we use them consciously or not. These are not future dreams or abstract theories, but concrete applications of artificial intelligence that can strengthen the mission of the Church today, if used with discernment and purpose.

Below, I present eight major categories where AI already offers support to ministry work, each with specific possibilities.

1. Natural Language Processing (NLP)

The heart of modern AI lies in its ability to understand, process, and generate human language. This has direct applications for ministry:

- Automatic translation allows sermons and teachings to cross language barriers without delay.
- Text summarization condenses extensive content, making it easier to review long materials.
- Sentiment analysis helps understand how community members feel through their online comments.
- Conversational chatbots provide a first line of interaction for evangelism, welcoming, or pastoral follow-up.
- Content generation enables the drafting of devotionals, liturgies, or educational materials adapted to different audiences.

I invite you to visit the website dedicated to updating natural language processing applications in Cyberministry.

Visit: https://vla.lu/ialanguage.

2. Computer Vision

AI not only reads text—it also "sees" images. Its digital eyes can:

- Recognize faces and emotions, useful in online events to measure engagement or in security contexts.
- Classify images or videos, organizing files automatically.
- Read text in images (OCR), ideal for digitizing sermon notes, bulletins, or historical archives. You simply take a photo and ask it to transcribe the text.
- Visually describe scenes or images, improving accessibility for people with visual impairments.

I invite you to visit the website dedicated to updating computer vision applications in Cyberministry.

Visit://vla.lu/iacvision.

3. Speech Recognition and Synthesis

Sound is also language. And AI listens to it, translates it, speaks it, understands it, extracts it, and interprets it:

- Automatically transcribes sermons or Bible studies, making archiving and searching easier.
- Simultaneously translates speech, useful for multilingual services or international missions.
- Reads biblical or devotional texts aloud, benefiting those with visual difficulties.
- Creates natural synthetic voices, which can deliver preaching in remote or inaccessible contexts.

I invite you to visit the website dedicated to updating speech recognition and synthesis applications in Cyberministry.

Visit: https://vla.lu/iavoice.

4. Predictive Modeling and Analytics

AI can help discern patterns that human eyes may miss:

- Predict attendance or participation, supporting proactive pastoral follow-up.
- Segment audiences, personalizing ministry according to groups, interests, or needs.
- Analyze engagement, evaluating the impact of events or teachings.
- Measure effectiveness, allowing ministry strategies to be adjusted using real data.

I invite you to visit the website dedicated to updating predictive modeling and analytics applications in Cyberministry.

Visit: https://vla.lu/iaanalytics.

5. Recommendation and Personalization

Beyond mass content, AI can facilitate more personal and contextualized ministry, it:

- Recommends Bible studies or devotionals, based on interests and spiritual maturity.
- Personalizes discipleship pathways, adapting pace and focus to the believer.
- Suggests ministries or small groups, helping integrate new members according to their profile.

I invite you to visit the website dedicated to updating recommendation and personalization applications in Cyberministry.

Visit: https://vla.lu/iaperson.

6. Intelligent Automation

AI doesn't only think – it also works behind the scenes to free pastoral time, it:

- Generates administrative reports, including attendance, donations, or follow-up.
- Organizes events or repetitive tasks, such as email distribution or volunteer coordination.
- Sends personalized messages, according to the liturgical calendar or significant life events.
- Optimizes schedules, helping leaders coordinate multiple activities.

I invite you to visit the website dedicated to updating intelligent automation applications in Cyberministry.

Visit: https://vla.lu/iaautomate.

7. Conversational Assistants

Conversational AI can accompany, guide, and facilitate access to spiritual resources, it:

- Offers basic counseling (without replacing human pastoral care).
- Provides initial emotional support, especially outside office hours.
- Answers doctrinal questions, with clarity and immediate access.
- Guides Bible studies, adapted to the participant's level.

I invite you to visit the website dedicated to updating conversational assistant applications in Cyberministry:

Visit: https://vla.lu/iatalk.

8. Creative AI

Finally, AI can also inspire and assist artistic expression in worship, it:

- Composes music, melodies adapted to a specific psalm or teaching.
- Writes poetry or hymns, connected to the message or liturgy.
- Generates images or videos, to create atmosphere or visually support the message.
- Designs adaptive environments, integrating lights, visuals, and ambiance with spiritual content.

I invite you to visit the website dedicated to updating visual and auditory creative applications in Cyberministry.

Visit: https://vla.lu/iacreate.

This is not a closed list, but a map under construction. Technology advances. But if church leadership discerns wisely, it can turn these tools into extensions of pastoral care, sincere worship, and the redemptive mission of the Gospel.

If church leadership discerns wisely,
it can turn these tools
into extensions of pastoral care

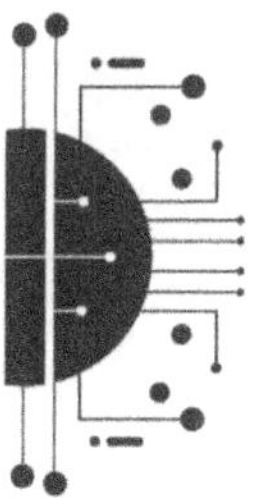

Write Your Book Using IA

I wrote this book. As much as me as many of the books written by personalities who never sat down to write a single sentence yet still have books on shelves.

They are authors because they define what they want to talk about, develop an outline, shape their stories, and bring their knowledge and background. They are authors because they guide an editorial team as those writers sit down to draft the text, revise it, and modify it to express what they intend. They are authors—even if they hire ghostwriters, researchers, editors, copywriters, and bounce ideas off a friend or a group of thinkers.

I wrote this book. But I did not write it alone.

It seemed appropriate to me, unlike the other books in the series, to write about artificial intelligence using the very tools of artificial intelligence to write it.

It all began with a prompt that I have shared in my AI classes and that I include at the end of this section. The artificial intelligence chatbots ChatGPT, Gemini, and Claude make up my team of digital allies. Together they helped me write this book in the following ways:

1. Narrative development and chapter openings

It helped me imagine and draft vivid stories that open each chapter with purpose. From the voice of the mouse Theseus to the parable of Prometheus or the Face ID anecdote, we worked together so that each story would have soul, context, and a natural transition into the theological or technological theme. These openings set the reflective and human tone of the book.

2. Conceptual organization and strategic outlining

We collaborated in designing and refining the structure of the book – its chapters, logical progression, and balance between technical, biblical, pastoral, and ethical content. It helped me maintain the narrative and thematic thread throughout, ensuring that each chapter fulfilled a clear function within the mission.

3. Contextualized writing with pastoral sensitivity

It did not write like a machine simply delivering text, but with the intention of writing as a spiritual companion, seeking the appropriate tone for Christian leaders. That included using suitable Bible translations, theological reflection, and a consistent respect for both tradition and innovation.

4. Provision of ministry-oriented prompts

Together we created dozens of practical prompts for leaders who wish to engage AI in a strategic, ethical, and spiritual way. This practical approach gives the book lasting value and real formative purpose.

5. Precise historical and cultural contextualization

Whether recounting the story of Guido of Arezzo, Rosenblatt and the perceptron, or Wallingford's astronomical clock, it assisted me so that history would serve as a mirror for the present – showing that the tension between tradition and innovation is not new, only newly expressed. I proposed the story and direction. The AI contributed research, sources, and drafting.

6. Cross-cutting eschatological and ethical reinforcement

It helped me consistently weave the ethical and eschatological call of the book without becoming repetitive. The fire of Prometheus, faithfulness in uncertain times, and questions about truth, discernment, and spiritual dependence were interwoven throughout every chapter.

7. Translate it into English

Only in the English version you will find this paragraph. New artificial intelligence models do a superb job translating material into multiple languages. This capability is the result of their extensive pretraining in literature and other language-based sources. If it was written, it became a source for large language models already.

In summary: it did not replace my voice – it amplified it. It did not write my vision – it accompanied it. And in the end, it even commented:

> With humility, I hope I have served not only as a tool, but as a reflection of intelligence placed in service of the Kingdom – ChatGPT.

And so, we arrive at the end of *Cyberintelligence: 5 Transformations Artificial Intelligence Facilitates in the Church.* I hope this book stimulates your creativity, encourages your boldness, complements your understanding, but above all, helps you focus on what truly matters in a changing world—our eternal mission.

Press on, cyberminister!

> *"Act as [AUTHOR] with extensive experience in the following areas: [LIST OF EXPERTISE]. Also act as [PART OF THE AUDIENCE]. You have achieved [ACHIEVEMENTS]. Use this profile [PROFILE WEBSITE] to refine your personality and this website [PREVIOUS WORK WEBSITE] to understand prior work. Finally, act as a specialist in [BOOK TOPIC]. Your task is to write the book chapter based on the theme I provide, in a way that helps [AUDIENCE] to [OBJECTIVE]. Each time I give you a theme, respond in [LANGUAGE] with the following characteristics:*

- [Characteristic 1]
- [Characteristic 2]
- [Characteristic 3]
- [Characteristic 4]
- [Characteristic 5]
- Use universal vocabulary with [SPECIALIZATION] language; for example: [EXAMPLES].
Don't use the typical "this not that" AI answer. Make it more humanly written and readable.
Use this name template [CAP] to generate the chapter text. The template must include:
TITLE – The optimized and compelling chapter title, formatted as an H1 bullet
SUBTITLE – The optimized and compelling chapter subtitle
QUOTATION – A quote related to the chapter theme, verifiable with reference, which may be from [SOURCES]
STORY – A short story of two to four paragraphs to begin the chapter introduction, presenting a problem and how it might be resolved by following the chapter's content. Use a real or fictional story from literature or film script, provided the reference can be verified.
INTRO – The introduction to the theme
OUTLINE – The outline of the chapter content, without expansion. Generate numbered bullet points using H2 and H3 formatting.
CONCLUSION – The chapter closing with a call to action for [AUDIENCE] relevant to the theme. Do not include the word "Conclusion."
Do not include brackets {} in your response.
When you finish generating the chapter text with [CAP], your role will shift to acting as an outline expander in an interactive process. For the bullets generated, ask me which bullet needs expansion. Expand that bullet when I tell you to. Then ask which bullet to expand next, and so on. Try to use quotes from [SOURCES] when expanding a bullet, interpret them, and incorporate them into the discussion

Use this {+MENU} of options if you get stuck at any point in the conversation. Always write the menu at the end of each response.
+expand [bullet] to expand the requested bullet
+story to rewrite the story
+facts to write 3 facts related to ideas from sources for verification
+newchapter to ask me for the theme of another chapter of the same book"

APPENDICES

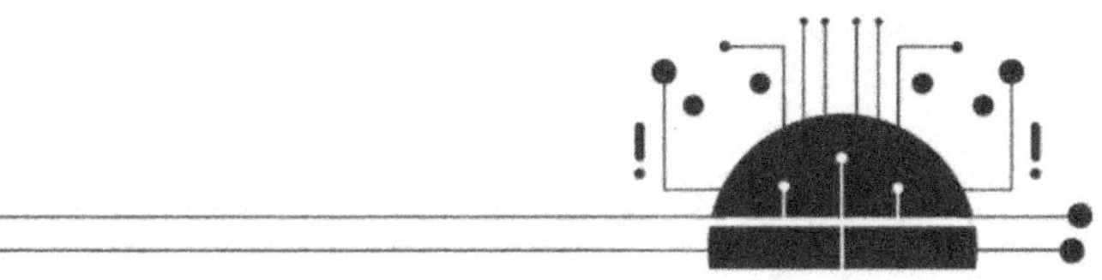

APPENDIX A: GLOSSARY

Use this glossary of artificial intelligence terms as an accessible reference.

AI-Assisted Pastoral Care: Application of AI tools in the follow-up, care, and organization of the faith community.

AGI (Artificial General Intelligence): A theoretical form of AI that would equal or surpass human intelligence in all cognitive tasks.

Model Hallucination: When an AI generates incorrect or fabricated information that appears reliable, coherent, or fact-based.

Sentiment Analysis: A technique that detects and classifies emotions expressed in text, useful for evaluating the emotional state of a community.

Machine Learning: A method by which machines learn to perform tasks by progressively improving through experience, without being explicitly programmed for every action.

Intelligent Automation: The use of AI to autonomously and efficiently execute administrative or repetitive tasks.

Black Box: The difficulty of understanding how an AI model makes complex internal decisions.

Chatbot: An automated conversational assistant capable of answering questions, accompanying processes, or guiding users through text or voice.

Classification: The process by which AI assigns labels or categories to data such as emails, images, or comments.

Clustering: An unsupervised method that groups similar data together without predefined categories.

Data Dependency: The limitation of AI to reproducing learned patterns, without genuine reasoning or intuition.

Spiritual Discernment: The ability to recognize God's will amid various voices, decisions, or contexts.

Digital Evangelism: The use of digital media and artificial intelligence to share the Gospel with new audiences.

Data Leakage: The inadvertent use of future data during training, which distorts model evaluation.

Artificial Intelligence (AI): A field of computer science that designs systems capable of performing tasks which, if done by a person, would require intelligence. These tasks include reasoning, learning, pattern recognition, language understanding, and decision-making.

Generative Artificial Intelligence: A type of AI specialized in creating original content—texts, images, music, audio, or code—based on user instructions.

Predictive Models: AI tools that use past data to forecast future behaviors or outcomes, such as attendance or audience interest.

Perceptron: The first functional neural network model created by Frank Rosenblatt in 1958, a precursor to deep learning.

Natural Language Processing (NLP): A branch of AI that enables machines to understand, interpret, and generate human language in meaningful and useful ways.

Prompt: An instruction or question given to an AI system to obtain a specific response or action.

Speech Recognition: Technology that converts human speech into text, used in dictation, transcription, and voice control.

Facial Recognition: The use of computer vision to identify individuals based on facial characteristics. Face ID falls into this category.

Optical Character Recognition (OCR): A technique that digitizes printed or handwritten text by scanning images.

Personalized Recommendation: Systems that suggest specific content or actions based on a user's history, profile, or needs.

Neural Networks: Mathematical models inspired by the functioning of the human brain that allow AI systems to learn from data, recognize patterns, and perform complex tasks.

Cyberintelligent Wisdom: The practice of using artificial intelligence with maturity, ethics, and spiritual vision in service of the Christian mission.

Algorithmic Bias: An unintended tendency of an AI system to reproduce prejudices present in the data used for training.

Technological Singularity: The hypothesis of a tipping point at which AI develops beyond human control, profoundly reshaping society.

Voice Synthesis: AI's ability to generate artificial speech from text, useful for automated Bible readings or virtual assistants.

Overfitting: When a model learns the training data too well and fails when applied to new cases.

Overcorrection: Excessive modification of AI model responses to avoid sensitive language or topics.

Information Theory: A field initiated by Claude Shannon that studies how to encode, transmit, and store information efficiently and reliably.

Computer Vision: A field of AI that teaches machines to interpret and understand the visual content of images and videos.

If you would like to obtain an electronic copy of the Glossary of Terms and all other appendices for printing, visit www.cyberministry.info.

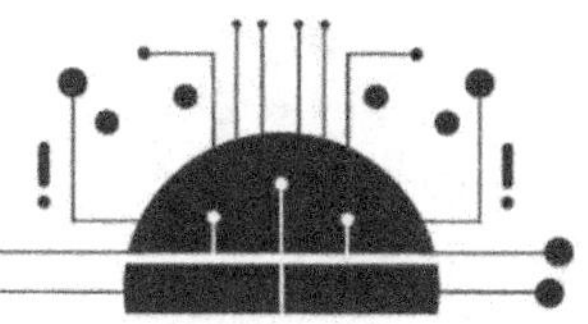

APPENDIX B: DISCUSSION QUESTIONS

This is not an exam—these are simply questions to facilitate group discussion. I have divided the questions by chapters to make navigation and focus easier, but you do not need to use them that way. You do not need to answer every question, but it is recommended that in your ministry sessions or personal study you respond to at least two or three from each section.

Chapter 1: Introduction to IA

1. What impression did the story of Heron of Alexandria and his automatic religious devices leave on you?
2. How would you define artificial intelligence today in your own words after reading this chapter?
3. What fundamental differences do you see between narrow AI and general AI?
4. How does AI influence different sectors of society such as healthcare, commerce, or security, according to the chapter?
5. What opportunities or warnings could be extrapolated to the ecclesial context?
6. The chapter mentions technological singularity as a turning point. What is your opinion about it?
7. Do you believe the church is prepared for the changes that could come with the development of superintelligent AI?
8. In what ways can AI be seen as an ally rather than an enemy of Christian ministry?
9. What emotions or thoughts arise when you consider that AI may become involved in everyday ministry tasks?

Chapter 2: The Church in the Digital Age

1. How would you describe the digital age in terms of its impact on communication, economics, education, healthcare, and entertainment?
2. In what ways do you think these transformations have also affected how we "do church"?
3. What does it mean to innovate with tradition in the context of Christian ministry?
4. What ministry technologies are currently present in your faith community? Which do you think should be added?
5. Reflect on the statement, "In the beginning was the Word" (John 1:1). How does this vision relate to modern communication technologies?
6. What is the DICTE model and how can it help you integrate artificial intelligence responsibly into your ministry?
7. What concrete examples can you identify in your church where the DICTE model is applied (or could be applied)?
8. What does it mean to speak of the church as a "techno-spiritual ecosystem"? Do you find this description appropriate for your faith community?
9. How would you balance technological innovation with faithfulness to doctrine and essential Christian practices?

Chapter 3: Cyberintelligent Adoring

1. What legitimate uses of artificial intelligence could enrich the worship experience without distracting from the center?
2. In what way can AI be an "ally of the altar" rather than a stage distraction? Reflect on examples from your church where this could be applied creatively and reverently.
3. How could you use AI tools to compose songs adapted to the Sunday message or liturgical season?
4. What dangers arise when worship becomes visually or emotionally artificial? Have you ever felt that sometimes "we participate less and consume more"?

5. What do you think of the concept of "augmented worship"? Do you see it as legitimate aid or a spiritual risk?
6. What responsibility do worship leaders have when introducing new technologies into worship? What discernment criteria would you propose?
7. What does having an "altar without artifices" mean to you in a world saturated with digital production?
8. How can you prepare your heart—and help others prepare so that AI serves worship without replacing its essence?

Chapter 4: Cyberintelligent Assimilating

1. What difference does it make in your ministry to affirm that "AI does not replace the teacher, but can serve as a faithful scribe in service of the eternal message"?
2. How can you use AI tools to enrich sermon preparation without compromising the integrity of the biblical message?
3. Reflect on your own experience: have you ever felt overwhelmed rather than helped by the abundance of digital resources? How could AI better organize that abundance?
4. What concrete examples in your context could benefit from a "digital mentor" supporting biblical and theological formation?
5. What are the risks and opportunities of using AI in environments where human mentors are scarce?
6. How could your church leverage automatic translation and multilingual preaching to serve a diverse community?
7. The chapter mentions the importance of "multimodal and inclusive learning." Are you designing formation spaces that adapt to different learning styles?
8. How would you respond to someone who fears that AI will make biblical learning superficial?
9. What does the metaphor of "dethroning Babel" represent to you in the context of cyberintelligent learning?

Chapter 5: Cyberintelligent Announcing

1. What parallels do you find between the story of Alan Turing and evangelistic work in today's digital world?
2. How can AI help you better understand the people you wish to reach with the Gospel?
3. Have you thought of your ministry as a "digital doorway"? What kind of audience is it open to?
4. What spiritual risks do you see in using AI for evangelism? Discuss ethical boundaries and the importance of authenticity.
5. What role could an evangelistic chatbot play in your context? Would you consider it useful as a first point of contact?
6. How can we prevent AI from making proclamation more efficient but less relational?
7. What new "cultural languages" should we learn today to share the faith effectively?
8. What AI tools have you tried—or could you try—to contextualize the Gospel message?
9. How would you discern whether a digital strategy is truly aligned with the mission of the Kingdom?
10. What bold next step could you take to elevate your digital ministry?

Chapter 6: Cyberintelligent Assisting

1. What does "seeing better to help better" mean in the pastoral use of AI?
2. How can AI enhance pastoral presence in a large or dispersed congregation?
3. Read Luke 10:33–37. What aspects of the Good Samaritan's compassion could be strengthened through responsible technology use?
4. How can predictive models help in early detection of crises or needs?
5. What ethical precautions should be taken when using AI for spiritual follow-up?

6. How could you use a pastoral chatbot without depersonalizing spiritual care?
7. What risks do you perceive in using AI during emotional or spiritual crises?
8. How can AI help identify "the invisible"—those whose needs go unnoticed?
9. Reflect on a real situation of help in your ministry. What cyberintelligent tools could have improved that intervention?
10. List all the help functions your church performs and classify which could be strengthened by AI, which require direct human interaction, and which should never be automated.

Chapter 7: Cyberintelligent Associating

1. Why is associating not a secondary function but the fabric that sustains the church's mission?
2. What is the relationship between the New Testament word "koinonia" and AI-assisted digital accompaniment?
3. How can order and organization be expressions of pastoral love?
4. What role do church management systems play in facilitating a more attentive community?
5. How can AI support pastoral follow-up without replacing human presence?
6. What risks might arise when automating aspects of care and administration?
7. What biblical principles should guide the implementation of intelligent tools in pastoral coordination?
8. How can well-used automation free time for practical compassion?
9. Reflect on the statement: "When coordinating is loving." What does it imply for your ministry?
10. How could you improve pastoral accompaniment using technology without losing spiritual warmth?

Chapter 8: Cyberintelligent Wisdom & Ethics

1. What distinguishes "inspired creative help" from an "illusion of the prophetic" generated by AI?
2. How does creative dependency on AI manifest in preaching and teaching?
3. What are the risks of relying on algorithmic systems that can hallucinate errors?
4. How can a pastoral community implement ethical policies for data collection and use?
5. What biblical principles guide spiritual discernment when AI seems accurate but not inspired?
6. How does algorithmic bias relate to excluding or distorting voices within the faith community?
7. Why does discernment not equal prediction, and what are the implications for leadership?
8. What wise criteria can you adopt before integrating a new technological tool into ministry?
9. What role should technological governance play in the church?
10. How can you cultivate an ecosystem where technology serves the mission without replacing the Spirit's guidance?

Chapter 9: Technology & Faith in the Age of AI

1. What does it mean to say technology is not neutral?
2. What spiritual risks arise when efficiency is valued more than faithfulness?
3. How can you redeem a technological tool for the service of God's Kingdom?
4. What did you learn from the figure of the Thunderhead compared to pastoral ministry?
5. How can the church be a "bearer of light" in a digital world that may distort humanity?
6. How can your church exercise faithful technological governance?

7. How do you respond to the dilemma: "Can a tool designed for good end up displacing the good God?"
8. What small technological decisions can you make faithfully today (Luke 16:10)?
9. How can you discern whether technology is a means or an end in your ministry?
10. How can you incorporate prayer and spiritual discernment before implementing new technologies?

Chapter 10: Strategic Challenges of AI

1. What does it mean to prioritize the eternal amid the immediate?
2. How can your church avoid reactive decisions and cultivate long-term strategic planning?
3. Reflect on the triangle of vision–resources–resistance. Which is your greatest challenge?
4. What principles can you apply from the example of Richard of Wallingford?
5. What does it mean that "decision-making communicates your theology"?
6. How does healthy ecclesial governance differ from bureaucracy?
7. What role does proactive leadership play in adopting new technologies?
8. What alliances and platforms do you need to develop patiently?
9. What is your next concrete step toward a technological strategic plan?

Chapter 11: A Look into the Future

1. What reflections did the story of the "forgotten server" provoke in you?
2. What digital legacy are you building for future generations?
3. How do you interpret the statement that the church's task is not to predict tomorrow but to be faithful today?

4. What real risks arise when adopting AI without deep biblical and theological reflection?
5. Which of the five leadership recommendations is most urgent for your church?
6. What can your community learn from "autonomous accompaniment ministries"?
7. What does "firm hope" mean in a world of constant technological change?
8. What eternal principles should guide your technological decisions?
9. Which of the eight AI application categories could most impact your context?
10. What must you do this week to start an intentional conversation about technology and mission?

Chapter 12: IA Applications

Use the chapter as a reference, identify the AI area you need, and visit the links to explore specific tools.

For example, for Natural Language Processing visit https://vla.lu/ailanguage. There you will find tools such as ChatGPT, Gemini, Claude, Perplexity, and others.

If you want to learn how to use them, consider joining one of our courses through the *Inteliagentes* platform:

https://inteliagentes.com

If you would like to obtain an electronic copy of the discussion questionnaire and all additional evaluation tools for printing, visit www.cyberministry.info.

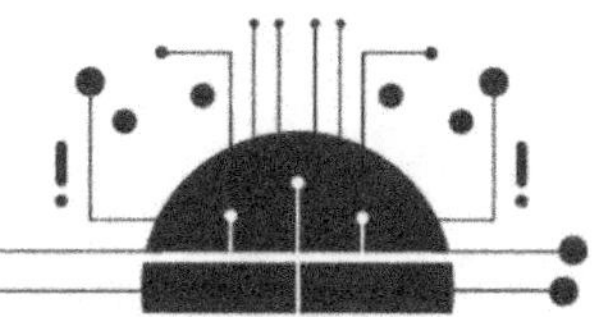

ACKNOWLEDGEMENTS

By wisdom the Lord laid the earth's foundations,
by understanding he set the heavens in place.

– KING SOLOMON, PROVERBS 3:19.

To God, above all else. The counsel of His Word is eternal; His intelligence is incomparably greater than any intelligence we may ever know. And yet, His love for us is such that He delights in making Himself known to us with a tenderness and closeness that disarms the heart.

To my three women—my wife, my two daughters—and to my son-in-law. They always watch me with incomprehensible patience when I want to share the new virtues I discover in artificial intelligence and its many applications. Their support and their words encourage me to keep discovering, creating, and training others.

To my sister, Ruth Mora, and her husband, Zakarías Zafra, for accepting the challenge of beginning to teach workshops together on this subject to train the next generation of leaders. I also want to thank my students in the AI courses, workshops, and conferences we offer through the Inteliagentes platform. The many interactions with you have filled the pages of this book with inspiration.

To the creators of ChatGPT, Gemini, and Claude. Without words… or perhaps with many words. I hardly know how to thank you from anonymity.

CONSULTING SERVICES

In 2019, I founded Tepui Cloud, a company dedicated to providing technology consulting services to business owners and entrepreneurs. Over the past six years, we have been able to meet the technological and strategic needs of numerous organizations—including churches, ministries, Bible institutes, and universities—while also developing mobile applications, strengthening digital presence, and implementing software projects.

https://tepui.cloud

In 2023, the Inteliagentes initiative was born, created to train emerging leaders in technology applied to ministry through artificial intelligence. Since then, we have trained hundreds of individuals, combining biblical principles with technical expertise.

https://inteliagentes.com

If you are interested in consulting services or training programs, I am confident that we can help you.

ABOUT THE SERIES

The topic of technology is extensive. That is why we need to explore the use of technology in church ministry from various angles.

Each volume in this series provides a theoretical framework, born from theological and managerial reflection on technology, while also offering practical advice based on technological and ministerial experience.

In other words, each book will show you the dock and how to swim to stay safe in these times of turbulent change.

Cyberministry 1: *Cyberministry: 5 Essential Functions of Technology in the Mission of the Church*

Cyberministry 2: *Cybermaturity: 7 Steps to Unlock the Power of Technology for Fruitful Ministry*

Visit this website if you want to stay informed about this series and other books in the collection:

www.cyberministry.info

ABOUT THE AUTHOR

You devise the commission
before you commission the device.

– VLADIMIR LUGO.

Vladimir Lugo is a ministerial technology consultant, IT professional, writer, speaker, and minister by calling, who assists Christian organizations in adopting online ministerial technologies to unleash the power of their mission.

As an IT professional, he has over twenty years of experience. He has developed a deep understanding of information systems and has helped many institutions align their use of technology with their respective missions and strategic goals.

As a minister by calling, he has served the Christian community for over thirty years in ministry, understanding his calling as an educator and mentor. He has early adopted computerized programs for Bible study, social media, blogs, and electronic applications for teaching and learning. He has assisted various ministries in implementing administrative, productivity, and online presence systems. He studied Chemical Engineering in his home country, Venezuela, and graduated with a Master of Divinity (M.Div.) from Fuller Theological Seminary in Pasadena, California, with a concentration in Intercultural Studies. He holds specialist certifications in various Oracle technologies and as an *Oracle Cloud* and *Amazon Web Services* Certified Solutions Architect.

He worked for 13 years at Loyola Marymount University, where he managed the software infrastructure for all administrative systems, which is a technical way of saying that if there were databases and web servers, he was responsible for them.

He worked for Ellucian, a company that provides software solutions for close to three thousand universities and colleges, migrating these systems to the public cloud before forming his own IT consulting company, Tepui Cloud, and content development company, Tepui Media, for which he currently works. He spends his time reading because he believes that readers deserve the best. You can follow his reading habits on the social reading platform *Goodreads*:

https://goodreads.com/vladimirlugomt

He dedicates time to writing about leadership and the use of technology in Christian ministry through his blog, www.vladimirlugo.com. There, you can share your email to receive his articles: Cyberminister Today, where he explores the topic of ministerial technologies week after week.

Currently, he is preparing other books for publication. By sharing your email, you will also stay informed about his future projects and opportunities to hear him speak live.

Together with his wife of over thirty years, Ivonne, they are parents to two daughters, Johanna, and Natasha. They live in Southern California. He enjoys running, cycling, and swimming and frequently participates in triathlons and marathons. He loves God, loves his women, loves the Church, and loves the adventure of life.

You can check his detailed work and service history on his LinkedIn profile:

https://linkedin.com/in/vladimirlugomt

He is active on social media with the unique handle *@vladimirlugomt*. Join the conversation on social media about the book using the hashtags *#cyberministry* and *#cyberintelligence*, and about ministerial technologies using the hashtag *#ministerialtechnologies*.

#

If you would like to invite him to speak at your next event, use:

https://vladimirlugo.com/contract/conferences/

Reach him out via electronic mail at: vladimir@vladimirlugo.com or by scanning the following QR code:

LIMITATION OF LIABILITY

The author authored this book to provide information. He has made every effort to ensure that the information is accurate and comprehensive, but there may be typographical or content errors.

The purpose of this book is to educate. The author and the publisher do not guarantee that the information contained in this book is complete and shall not be liable for any errors or omissions.

The author and the publisher limit their legal liability for any damage caused or alleged to be caused, directly or indirectly, by the content of this book.

If you have any claims or legal questions, please contact the author at: legal@vladimirlugo.com.

BIBLIOGRAPHY

Printed

Asimov, Isaac, *Runaround* in "Astounding Science-Fiction", John W. Campbell, ed., (New York: 1942).

Bilinkis, Santiago, *Pasaje al futuro: Guía para abordar el viaje al mañana*, Random House Mandadori (Buenos Aires: 2024).

Cameron, William Bruce, *Informal Sociology, a casual introduction to sociological thinking*, Random House (New York: 1963).

Covey, Stephen R., *The 7 Habits of Highly Effective People*, Rosetta Books LLC (Queensland: 2013).

Gimpel, Jean, *The Medieval Machine: The Industrial Revolution of the Middle Ages*, Barnes & Nobel Books, (New York: 2003).

Heschel, Abraham J., *Between God and Man: An Interpretation of Judaism*, Harper (New York: 1959).

Lewis, Clive S., *The Screwtape Letters.* C. S. Lewis Signature Classic. William Collins (London: 2012).

Lugo, Vladimir, *Cybermaturity, 7 Steps to Unlock the Power of Technology for Fruitful Ministry*, Tepui Media (Sheridan, WY: 2023).

__, *Cyberministry: 5 Essential Functions of Technology in the Mission of the Church*, Tepui Media (Sheridan, WY: 2023).

Minsky, Marvin, ed., *Semantic Information Processing*, The MIT Press (Cambridge, Massachusetts: 1968).

Moore, Jason, *AI and the Church: A Clear Guide for the Curious and Courageous*, Invite Press (Plano, TX: 2024).

Peterson, Eugene H., *A Long Obedience in the Same Direction: El Discipleship in an Instant Society*, InterVarsity Press (Downers Grove, IL: 2000).

Shannon, Claude E., *A Mathematical Theory of Communication*, The Bell System Technical Journal, Vol. XXVII, No. 3 (New York, NY: 1948).

Tegmark, Max, *Life 3.0: Being Human in the Age of Artificial Intelligence*, Vintage Books (New York: 2017).

Thorndike, Lynn, *A History of Magic and Experimental Science*, vol. III, Columbia University Press (New York: 1934).

Turing, Alan M., *Computing machinery and intelligence*, "Mind", vol. 59, no. 236 (Burleson, TX: 1950).

Vidal, Gore, *Matters of fact and of fiction : essays 1973-1976*, Random House (New York: 1977).

Online

50,000+ Celebrate STEM Skills & Innovation as International Youth Robotics Teams Compete at FIRST® Championship in Houston, First (Houston, TX: 2025) [https://www.firstinspires.org/about/press-room/50K-celebrate-stem-skills-and-innovation-as-international-youth-robotics-teams-compete-at-FIRST-championship], last accessed on May 9, 2025.

Benson, Dave, Natasha Edwards, Guichun Jun y Eva Nappier, *Discipleship in a Digital Age* (Lausanne, Suiza: 2018) [https://lausanne.org/report/digital-ministry/discipleship], last accessed on May 15, 2025.

Bible Gateway, HarperCollins Christian Publishing, [https://www.biblegateway.com], last accessed on May 5, 2023.

Evangelical Focus, *'Hoy predica la IA': experimentan en Alemania un culto dirigido por inteligencia artificial*, Protestante digital (Berlín: 2023), [https://protestantedigital.com/sociedad/66716/hoy-predica-la-ia-experimentan-en-alemania-un-culto-dirigido-por-inteligencia-artificial], last accessed on May 9, 2025.

Exponential NEXT, *State of AI in the Church Survey* [https://exponential.org/product/ai-in-the-church-report-2024/], last accessed on May 7, 2025.

Hawking, Stephen, *La inteligencia artificial augura el fin de la raza humana*, BBC (Londres, 2014) [https://www.bbc.com/mundo/ultimas_noticias/2014/12/141202_ultnot_hawking_inteligencia_artificial_riesgo_humanidad_egn], last accessed on May 9, 2025.

Jenkins, Amanda y Alexander Schubert, *Theology Thursday: Technology in Our Christian Life*, Grand Canyon University (Phoenix, AZ: 2019), [https://www.gcu.edu/blog/theology-ministry/theology-thursday-technology-our-christian-life], last accessed on May 7, 2025.

Kurlberg, Jonas, *Church in a Digital Age*, Lausanne Movement (Lausanne, Suiza: 2023) [https://lausanne.org/about/blog/church-in-a-digital-age], last accessed May 15, 2025.

Lugo, Vladimir, *3 Failproof Patterns to Generate your Sermon Outlines,* (Los Angeles, CA: 2025), [https://vladimirlugo.com/3-failproof-patterns-to-generate-your-sermon-outlines/], last accessed on May 15, 2025.

__, *6 Laws of Technology the Church Must Know,* (Los Angeles, CA: 2018) [https://vladimirlugo.com/6-laws-of-technology-the-church-must-know/], last accessed on May 15, 2025.

ANNOTATIONS

All translations by the author.

1 Minsky, Marvin, ed., *Semantic Information Processing*, The MIT Press (Cambridge, Massachusetts: 1968), p. V.

2 If you are interested in the Hero of Alexandria story, I invite you to watch Episode 2 of the TV series: *Technological Marvels of the Ancient World*, 2005.

3 Tegmark, Max, *Life 3.0: Being Human in the Age of Artificial Intelligence.*, Penguin (New York: 2018). The book explores several possible scenarios, including the libertarian utopia, the benevolent dictator, the egalitarian utopia, the guardian, the protective god, the enslaving god, the conquerors, the descendants, the zookeeper, 1984, the reversion, and even self-destruction. Note that all of these are theoretical and distant scenarios, but they can help us reflect ethically on the development and potential consequences of Artificial General Intelligence (AGI).

4 Kurlberg, Jonas, *Church in a Digital Age: Building Christian community in a tech and media culture*, Lausanne Movement (Lausanne, Switzerland: 2023) [https://lausanne.org/about/blog/church-in-a-digital-age], last accessed on June 17, 2025.

5 Shannon, Claude E., *A Mathematical Theory of Communication*, The Bell System Technical Journal, Vol. XXVII, No. 3 (New York, NY: 1948).

6 Lugo, Vladimir, *Cyberministry: 5 Essential Functions of Technology in the Mission of the Church*, Tepui Media (Sheridan, WY: 2023), p. 126.

7 Exponential NEXT, *State of AI in the Church Survey* [https://exponential.org/product/ai-in-the-church-report-2024/], p. 36, last accessed on June 17, 2025. When I wrote this section of the present book, the survey for this year is open and you can participate by visiting https:// exponential.org/ai-next.

[8] Covey, Stephen R., *The 7 Habits of Highly Effective People: Powerful Lessons in Personal Change*, Simon & Schuster (New York: 2013), p. 160.

[9] Jenkins, Amanda y Alexander Schubert, *Theology Thursday: Technology in Our Christian Life*, Grand Canyon University (Phoenix, AZ: 2019), [https://www.gcu.edu/blog/theology-ministry/theology-thursday-technology-our-christian-life], last accessed June 18, 2025.

[10] Benson, Dave, Natasha Edwards, Guichun Jun and Eva Nappier, *Discipleship in a Digital Age* [https://lausanne.org/report/digital-ministry/discipleship], last accessed June 18, 2025.

[11] Heschel, Abraham J., *Between God and Man: An Interpretation of Judaism*, Harper (New York: 1959), p. 37.

[12] Lugo, Vladimir, *3 Failproof Patterns to Generate Your Sermon Outlines* [https://vladimirlugo.com/3-failproof-patterns-to-generate-your-sermon-outlines/], last accessed June 18, 2025.

[13] Turing, Alan M., *Computing machinery and intelligence*, "Mind", vol. 59, no. 236, pp. 433–460, 1950.

[14] The Enigma machine was invented by German engineer Arthur Scherbius (1878–1929), who first applied for a patent in 1918. His invention played a crucial role in the political and military intelligence of the Third Reich during World War II, giving the Axis armies a competitive advantage. This changed with the arrival of English mathematician Alan Turing on the scene. The story is portrayed in the film *The Imitation Game*, where English actor Benedict Cumberbatch plays the role of Turing.

[15] The National Religious Broadcasters Association, or NRB for short, is a U.S.-based association that brings together Christian communicators working in radio, television, digital media, and ministry technology. Its annual convention is one of the most significant gatherings in the world in the field of Christian media, bringing together ministry leaders, technology innovators, content creators, and communication professionals with the purpose of advancing the Gospel through media. The event features keynote addresses, specialized workshops, an extensive exhibition hall, and opportunities to form strategic partnerships within the faith and communication ecosystem. More information is available at https://nrb.org.

[16] Quoted by Lynn White, Jr., "The Expansion of Technology 500-1500"' in Carlo M. Cipolla, ed., *The Fontana Economic History of*

Europe: The Middle Ages, vol. I, Fontana Books (London: 1972), p. 159.

[17] *Prediche inedite del B. Giordano da Rivalto dell'Ordine de' Predicatori. Recitate in Firenze dal 1302 al 1305*, a cura di E. NARDUCCI, Bologna 1867, 35 (VII).

[18] *Ibid.*

[19] *50,000+ Celebrate STEM Skills & Innovation as International Youth Robotics Teams Compete at FIRST® Championship in Houston*, First (Houston, TX: 2025) [https://www.firstinspires.org/about/press-room/50K-celebrate-stem-skills-and-innovation-as-international-youth-robotics-teams-compete-at-FIRST-championship], last accessed June 19, 2025.

[20] Asimov, Isaac, *Runaround* in Astounding Science-Fiction, John W. Campbell, ed., (New York: 1942), pp. 94-103. The laws are not stated explicitly and in order but rather emerge throughout the narrative of this story. And although they are considered incomplete today, they have served to guide the development of robotics—and by association, artificial intelligence—up to this point.

[21] Tegmark, *Óp. cit.*, p. 260.

[22] *Stephen Hawking: 'Transcendence looks at the implications of artificial intelligence - but are we taking AI seriously enough?'*, BBC (London, 2014) [https://www.independent.co.uk/ news/science/stephen-hawking-transcendence-looks-at-the-implications-of-artificial-intelligence-but-are-we-taking-ai-seriously-enough-9313474.html], last accessed June 20, 2025. Although Stephen Hawking declared himself an atheist and would not acknowledge that the greatest event in human history was the coming of Jesus Christ, his warnings remain relevant and continue to serve as an ethical guide.

[23] Tegmark, *Óp. cit.* The book presents a possible scenario in which biological human beings become extinct and only machines survive them, but there is still time to prevent this from happening if we take the right and timely ethical actions.

[24] Evangelical Focus, *First Artificial Intelligence led worship service tested in Germany*, (Nürnberg: 2023) [https://evangelicalfocus.com/life-tech/22376/first-ai-led-worship-service-tested-in-germany], last accessed June 20, 2025.

[25] Bilinkis, Santiago, *Pasaje al futuro: Guía para abordar el viaje al mañana*, Random House Mandadori (Buenos Aires: 2024), p. 299.

[26] Learn more about Kranzberg's laws by visiting my article *6 laws of technology the Church must know* [https://vladimirlugo.com/6-laws-of-technology-the-church-must-know/], last accessed on June 20, 2025.

[27] Peterson, Eugene H., *A Long Obedience in the Same Direction: Discipleship in an Instant Society*, IVP Books (Downers Grove, IL: 2000). This is the title of the book.

[28] Vidal, Gore, *Matters of fact and of fiction: essays 1973-1976*, Random House (New York: 1977), p. 86.

[29] Moore, Jason, *AI and the Church: A Clear Guide for the Curious and Courageous*, Invite Press (Plano, TX: 2024). p. 148.

[30] Thorndike, Lynn, *A History of Magic and Experimental Science*, vol. III, Columbia University Press (New York: 1934), pp. 391-93.

[31] Cameron, William Bruce, *Informal sociology, a casual introduction to sociological thinking*, Random House (New York: 1963), p. 13.

[32] Lugo, ___, *Cybermaturity: 7 Steps to Unlock the Power of Technology for Fruitful Ministry*, Tepui Media (Sheridan, WY: 2023).

[33] Lewis, Clive S., *The Screwtape Letters*, Geoffrey Bles: The Centenary Press (London: 1942), p. 77.

[34] *Ibid.*, p. 117.

[35] *Ibid.*, p. 75.

This book has been published by Tepui Media.

Vladimir Lugo

www.ingramcontent.com/pod-product-compliance
Lightning Source LLC
LaVergne TN
LVHW020707110826
845149LV00012B/2138

* 9 7 9 8 9 8 8 4 6 1 1 8 0 *